# MORE OF GOD IN OUR LIVES & STORIES:

## THE POWER OF THE RESURRECTION

BY KIMBERLY GIBSON JOHNSON

✦

THIS BIBLE STUDY BELONGS TO

_____

_____

*More of God in Our Lives and Stories: The Power of the Resurrection*

© 2024 Kimberly Gibson Johnson

All rights reserved. No portion of this book may be reproduced by any means, graphic, electronic, or mechanical, including photocopying, recording, taping or by any information storage retrieval system without the written permission of the publisher except in the case of brief quotations embodied in critical articles and reviews.

Published by
Gibson, Johnson & Company, Inc.
P.O. Box 250646
Atlanta, GA 30325
kimberlygibsonjohnson.org

Designed by
Megan Inderrieden
meg-indy.com

ISBN: 978-1-7338718-2-2
Library of Congress Control Number: 2024906700

Unless otherwise noted, all Scripture references are from the New International Version edition, published by Zondervan Publishing House.

Copyright © 1973, 1978, 1984, 2011

Printed in the United State of America.
Gibson, Johnson & Company, Inc., June 24, 2024

# TABLE OF CONTENTS

| | |
|---|---|
| PREFACE | 3 |
| INTRODUCTION | 10 |
| I. PETER | 17 |
| PERSPECTIVE: THE SEARCH FOR MORE | 32 |
| II. ABRAHAM | 37 |
| PERSPECTIVE: HARDSHIP | 52 |
| III. RAHAB | 57 |
| PERSPECTIVE: CROSSING OVER | 72 |
| IV. ELIZABETH | 75 |
| PERSPECTIVE: BY FAITH | 90 |
| V. DEBORAH | 95 |
| PERSPECTIVE: WHO IS GOD | 110 |
| VI. PAUL | 115 |
| PERSPECTIVE: HOW GOD BECOMES THE MAIN | 130 |
| VII. MOSES | 133 |
| PERSPECTIVE: PRAYING | 148 |
| VIII. MARY MAGDALENE | 151 |
| PERSPECTIVE: COLLABORATION | 166 |
| IX. JOSHUA | 171 |
| PERSPECTIVE: GOD'S CALL IS TO KNOW HIM | 186 |
| X. DAVID | 189 |
| PERSPECTIVE: GOD'S PLAN FOR US | 204 |
| XI. ANNA | 207 |
| PERSPECTIVE: GOD IS ALWAYS WITH US | 222 |
| XII. LYDIA | 227 |
| PERSPECTIVE: MORE OF GOD IN OUR LIVES | 242 |
| FINAL THOUGHTS | 245 |

# A WORD OF APPRECIATION

*I am indebted to many friends and family members, who have encouraged me to write and teach this Bible Study, not the least of whom were the first readers and students to show up and participate enthusiastically in the initial classroom study. You know who you are. Thank you from the bottom of my heart!*

*The Rev. Dr. G. Gil Watson encouraged me very early on in the development and writing of the study. I think of our visit and your words to me often, Dr. Gil. Marty Michaud came along beside me to offer this study as part of Johnson Ferry Women's Ministry curriculum. I will forever be grateful for your walking the journey with me, praying for me as I taught, coordinating and facilitating our discussion groups, and joining with me in prayer for each member of the class to know God more deeply through the study. And special thanks to Johnson Ferry Women's Ministry! Megan, Meg Indy, you rock, my friend. I love the variety and depth of the art you produce. Your beautiful cover along with the inside text formatting make the presentation of this material a wonderful work of art.*

*Awed and humbled by you, the reader and student, participating in this study, I pray that each of us will grow in knowing God more and more as we read and study His word. To God be the glory!*

*Sincerely,*
*Kim*

# LET GOD BE GOD
## IN YOUR LIFE BY THE POWER OF THE RESURRECTION

God has written your story and mine. In collaborating with Him, the life He imagined for us unfolds. We do not know where we will end up, but He does. What if we were to live with a faith that enables us to go the next step with Him even when we want to do another, or even when we are afraid, or most importantly, when we are certain that the other would bring about our own desires.

What about the desires of our hearts? God knows them, and He is giving us new ones as we follow Him. It turns out that when we are letting God be God in our lives, He is transforming us from the inside out. In other words, His desires become our own. So, with each step, each choice we make in accordance with and in collaboration with Him, we have the faith we need to go the step, and the things for which we yearn are actually all met in Him.

Sometimes the pull in the other direction is so strong. What do we do? In order to discern, we must be in the word of God and also listening to what He says to us in our reading and in laying it out there to Him in prayer. It also helps if we have someone we can trust for wise counsel, who also is in the word of God and in prayer for us.

Choosing to follow Jesus is simple but not easy. Jesus knows this and knows the deep desires and the strong yearnings we have for this life journey. After all, He created us and knows our story from beginning to end. He has the best for each of us, and He is using the ones who follow Him for His purposes and plans for all the world to know Him.

It may not seem that what we choose has consequence, especially in the grand scheme, but it does. God has formed the hearts of all; He has plans greater than we imagine. The mystery of God is hidden until He reveals what He does for His purposes. Perhaps we will not know what a choice will mean in the kingdom of God, but He is shaping our hearts for His divine purpose; this is a huge deal and consequence for His kingdom.

The privilege of being a vessel of His choosing for His purposes and glory is too big to fathom; however, He has chosen us to display His love for all the world to see. If we walk forward with Him in the lead, He will take us where He wants us to go and use us to show His truth and love to the world. What better reason to let God be God in our lives!

**No good thing**
As followers of Jesus, we lack no good thing. The Lord does not withhold good things from us. He pursues us to give us good things, the best in Jesus. What is the good thing for which you yearn? Do you know that He knows about it? Are you His follower, and have you told Him about your desires for this life? His word teaches us and reminds us of the good things that He has in store for us. He chose us before the creation of the world. In addition, He created us for good works, which He planned for us before we were born.

In collaboration with Him as His children, we may live and work as He planned for His name so that others may know Him too. He has and desires good things for us; He gives only good things. The Lord is mighty to rescue us; His lovingkindness is forever for us. He never changes; the Lord is just, merciful, and kind. We are His heirs, and He is our Father. In Him is no darkness; He shows us the way. He is the way, the truth, and the life. The evil one comes to steal, kill, and destroy; yet, the Lord has come to give us life, life to the full in Him.

These are few of the good things that the Lord gives us in Jesus Christ. We cannot get to the end of the good things of God. Nor can we know all of them. It is on the journey with Him that we come to know Him more and more and have faith in the person and plans of Jesus Christ, our Lord and Savior. In His choosing us, we have a decision to make and that is to follow Him. If we do not choose, we have made the choice not to follow Him. However, when we do, His goodness and mercy follow us all the days of our lives and into eternity with Him. This is the good news of Jesus Christ with all good things to follow.

**Psalm 84:11**
For the Lord God is a sun and shield; the Lord bestows favor and honor; no good thing does he withhold from those whose walk is blameless.

> Redemption is what the Lord offers each of us through Jesus Christ. He redeems our lives through the sacrifice of His Son so that we may live now and eternally with Him. Redeeming what has been lost is what the Lord does in each of our lives when we choose to follow Him. We are lost until Jesus is known to us and we have fellowship with Him:
>
> Redemption, God's rescue of us, is for God's glory and for our good
>
> When we say "yes" to Him and His rescue, we follow Him
>
> Through Jesus, we are right with God
>
> We are set free from sin's hold on us
>
> We are known as His "chosen ones"
>
> With a relationship with Him, we have a sense of belonging
>
> There will be hardship and suffering in our lives
>
> In the suffering, God reveals a unique story in each of our lives for God's glory for the world to know Him

**Psalm 34:10**
The lions may grow weak and hungry, but those who seek the Lord lack no good thing.

**The deep place where God meets us by the power of the resurrection**
The deep, deep place where God meets us to love us with His unfailing love, to comfort us with His lovingkindness, to relieve us from fear and anxiety, to free us from what is holding us back or binding us up, to hold us close in order to shield us from harm, and to meet us to show us how to release us from carrying things we are not designed to carry is where He reveals to us our great need for Him and also helps us to receive what He has already given us in Jesus. This is what the Lord does when He shows up in our need to meet our need. In Him is every counterpart to each need we have.

What place within you is needing the Lord's touch? He is pursuing you for more of Him. We can never get to the end of Him. What are some of the themes in your life story? Where has He shown up?

Are there seasons of sorrow and distress which have similar themes to other difficult times in your life? Might these inhibit you from knowing more of God Himself, the fullness of God? What has been stolen from you? Have relationships been damaged? What do you no longer desire to be healed because it would hurt too much to want it? Has this dream or hope been squelched?

The Lord pursues us to fill these places with Himself in our hearts and life stories, the places we have pushed back in the crevices of our heart of doubt and destruction and abandonment. He is the Lord of lovingkindness, mercy, and rescue; He is our Abba Father, the One who answers when we call.

> The Psalmist seeks God and asks Him to show us the wonder of His great love (Psalm 17:7a). We are going to be doing the same as we go through this study for the context of seeking and knowing God more and more by:
>
> *Asking God to help us through the power of the Holy Spirit to see and experience the wonder of His great love in His greatest story of who He is, the author of all, including our stories and those of our ancestors*
>
> *Seeking to know Him more and more*
>
> *Observing and experiencing who God is and what He does, the wonder of it all*
>
> *Knowing God's attributes, His character, His unfailing love for us, His creation, made for His purposes, plans, and glory, for all the world to know Him*
>
> His wonder is more than we can imagine, and His word is full of His unfailing love for His children through His pursuit of them for relationship with Him.

Sometimes we have recurring themes because there has been a desire or dream that surfaces and the Lord wants us to bring it to Him, to know Him more through it. Other times it is a hurt or struggle brought about by loss or betrayal through which we see all other things, some harmful and some not. The Lord would have us bring it to Him in order for Him to show us how much He loves us and has for us in it.

Nothing is happenstance. There is nothing that the Lord does not know. All things come through the sovereign hand of God. He allows us to hurt and to struggle so that we may have more of Him. He has given us all of Himself, and He wants us to receive it in full.

In the moments of deep longing and turning to God, He opens our hearts and minds to hear Him. It is in our place of great need and humility that the Lord meets us. Our hearts are ready to receive that which God has pursued us—His rescue into more of Him. This is the main thrust of the Bible study.

Identifying who God is with the help of the Holy Spirit in each biblical person's story gives us an understanding of who He is in our own individual stories as they fit into the Lord's greatest story.

**Context as we study God's word by the power of the resurrection**

Let's talk about context. We are going to take a look at many scriptures throughout this study and ask the Holy Spirit to guide us into truth as we read them, truth about who God is and what He does with and for His chosen ones, His children. While we are studying, we will be asking several questions and asking the Lord to help us as we discern what He has for us during this time in His word.

The context of a scripture gives us a lot of information about the time and place and the people with whom the text is referring. As readers and students of the text, we are able to discern who the person or people are and how they live and whether they are following God or other gods. A lot of the time it may seem quite foreign to us. Context matters, and we are going to see this as we study each Biblical person. The children of God under the old covenant experienced and knew God in a different way from those under the new covenant, who met Jesus or who were taught by those who knew Him. We are also going to see that God never changes. His character is the same yesterday, today, and forever. The manner in which God shows up in our lives and the means He uses for each one of us to follow Him are unique. An easy thing to fall into is reading the scripture through our own lens, but we would like to read His word with a unique lens, which He will give us as we study. We must not narrow our focus on the person or the ways in which we compare ourselves to the person we study; there is a place for this, and it is appropriate, of course, for understanding and learning purposes. However, our study's focus is on God Himself.

In His word, we will see themes in a person's life just as there are themes in our own. As the Lord gives us a new view of who He is through the context and themes of a particular Biblical person, let's allow Him also to give us a new view of our own lives and purpose in Him.

---

**What is the Holy Spirit teaching us?**

*Giving us a new view – His perspective*

*Reminding us that He loves us*

*Pursuing us with hard things to allow us the choice to lean on Him*

*Shaping us into more of Him in our lives and stories*

*Hearing and guiding us when we pray*

*Rescuing us from our sin and harmful ways*

*Giving us insight into His word today, each day*

---

**Ask yourself the following:**

*What in our study can we identify with today?*

*What do we want to hear from the Lord today?*

*Are we listening?*

*Are we in His word?*

*What help from the Lord are we waiting upon?*

*When have you asked Him for help?*

*How do you pray?*

**Releasing our past failures and sin to our Father God in Jesus Christ by the power of the resurrection**
I am reminded of who God is in Psalm 51; He is merciful and kind, not remembering our sin, but giving us a clean slate — a pure heart to know Him and respond to Him in gratitude and to lean into Him, who sustains us with His extravagant love and grace. As we receive this amazing love He has given us in Jesus Christ, He also gives us hearts to praise Him for who He is and what He has done for us.

Being drawn to the key verses of "create in me a clean heart," the Holy Spirit opens me up to know that He has already given it; thus, I am walking this road with a pure heart because of what Jesus has done for me. Nothing I have done or not done has given me this heart, but Jesus. Only He is worthy of praise! He says to move past the mistake, the failure, the sin that so easily hinders me from this new life, this journey with Him. Let it go; He has it all. The Lord knows it all, and the release of it back to Him is an act of faith. The broken or contrite heart is also an act of faith; He has given me a softer heart to know Him, to accept the things that have not been and the things that I have not been in order to receive the new person He has created me to be.

I know Him, and because I do, His heart is within mine. I cannot do this on my own, but only through Him in me. His way becomes mine; His love, His heart, and the extravagance of it all are mine for the journey.

Praising Him comes into focus because He is the life for which we yearn. Only with Him in view will His rest come and give me the release I so desire from all that is in the past. Have you given Him yours? The failures, the sin that so easily entangles? When you do, He will give you a new song to sing.

---

**The Past**
Looking through the lens of who God is as the author of our lives and stories, we may see how He has come along beside us and guided us through many hard things in our lives, covered us with His blessings, and brought into our lives joy and comfort. Sometimes, the past is a mysterious combination of a circuitous path and an unveiling of "what do I make of this?" Yet, we know the truth of the character of God and His lovingkindness toward each of His children, you and me. What if we were to take a look back with the Holy Spirit's guidance, and not shine a bright light on our messes, but keep our attention on the ways the Lord met us during these years? He will give us a new view. He doesn't change our decisions or keep us free from consequences, but He does provide and protect and love us despite our sin and messes.

---

**Trusting God in the difficult by the power of the resurrection**
Jesus died for us to know Him and live with Him forever. How are we going to respond to this news? Trusting God with the most difficult things—the innermost hurts, the deepest wounds, and the gravest sin, is what He asks of us. Because we cannot do it on our own without His help, He causes us to come to Him for mercy. And when we do, He gives us what we need to know Him, His forgiveness, His heart of lovingkindness, and His almighty power to grow, heal, hope, and live in this new day. What is He asking you to release to Him at this point in time? How are you going to give it to Him? If you are not choosing to give it to Him, why not?

Do you need forgiveness, healing, power, love, or hope today? I need all for every moment of every day; however, I don't necessarily ask the Lord. I talk to Him about a lot of things, but sometimes I hold the hard ones back. Is it because I have asked already? Could be. Is it because I don't think the Lord will answer, or answer in the way I want Him to answer? Probably. Or is it because I am spouting off all the lesser things to Him like a laundry list when the main thing is still the main thing. He wants to hear about all of it, but most importantly, He knows that I/we need to release it to Him.

> **The Present**
> Let's take a look at the provision of our Maker and Savior Jesus Christ through the lens of who He is and what He does for His children. The truth in God's word describes His nature and His ways; He does not change. If He took care of His children throughout history, He is still taking care and leading them now. What about you? How do you see His hand and His love today? Have you asked Him to guide you into His truth. He will and He does! It is who He is.

We are not designed to carry heavy or hard things. Sometimes He takes the heavy things from us; sometimes He carries us through the heavy and hard times. And then often, if we let Him into the hard place, He gives us a new view of Himself, the One who calls us by name to know Him, the Lord of all mankind, our Savior, Creator, and Redeemer, Jesus Christ. It is in this place and time, we make a step of faith, and it is true and wonderful and a new thing. When this happens, we heal a bit, we hope a bit more, and we certainly have new life within, the life He imagined for us. With this, He becomes more; we know Him more; and we have catapulted to a new and spacious place, more of Him in our lives and stories.

We experience what He died for us to have, peace and rest in Him, to be able to stay close to Him, because He created it this way. Are there places in your life where you need the peace of the Lord? Or rest? Might you respond to the Lord with a plea that you would like to release something difficult to Him, something that has been weighing heavy on you for a long time? He is waiting for you to receive His lovingkindness, which He has already given once and for all in Jesus Christ. He is calling out to you in your distress, running after you to rescue you. How might you respond now?

> **The Future**
> The Lord of the universe, Jesus Christ, gives us hope for the future. His hand to guide and protect and fill our lives with His grace and truth is always present in the Holy Spirit. How are you taking hold of His truth and grace? What might you do differently today to turn your focus onto who He is? Might this perspective allow you to change your course from thinking and moving in the direction of your own to the path He has set for you. This path is the one He authored before you were born. He has created you for His purposes so that the world will know Him. What an honor and a privilege that God gives us to have a story within the greatest story, His!

**What is it that the Lord wants from us by the power of the resurrection**
*To come. To listen. To thank Him. To praise Him. To give up our own mindset to allow Him in. To allow our hearts to be redeemed by His, in other words, allow His rescue. To be willing to follow His lead every moment of every day.* We will fail, but He is also the One who makes it possible for us to come. He is our teacher and reminder of what He teaches as we come to Him. As we place our effort on coming to Him, in other words, trusting Him, He multiplies the faith He has given us in the first place.

The Lord does not need anything from us. He wants a relationship with us, which first starts as we choose to respond to His call. He initiates always. And He gives us the ability to turn around toward Him. It is His way, a most beautiful and mysterious one. Only His could be this powerful and merciful, and also kind and generous.

Jesus calls us to come. As we do, He gives us the measure of faith, courage, and strength to do so. Walking with Him is the way, the truth, and the life. The life He has given in Jesus is what He wants us to receive. Let us come to follow, praise, and thank Him for the marvelous thing He has done!

---

**Author's Note**

*God the Father, Jesus, and the Holy Spirit have always been; they were together at creation and before. So, as you will notice in this study, we talk about how the Power of the Resurrection has always been in existence too, just as the Father, Son, and Holy Spirit. Sometimes, we lose sight of this as we study the scriptures within their own context and setting. God sends the Holy Spirit in the Old Testament, whereas after Jesus' ascends to be with the Father, He sends the Holy Spirit to indwell His people on earth as in the New Testament, He lives within and gives His people the capacity to walk with Him on the journey of life. The power of the resurrection is the power the Lord exerted to raise Jesus from the dead. The Lord, who has been, is, and is to come, reigns in love and power. He has always had the power of the resurrection and has always had the plan to send His only Son to die and live again for us to know Him and live with Him. Our study highlights that it is by His power, we live and walk with Him, as have all who have lived and gone before us and will after us. The people of God have His power; it is only by His power that we may live out the stories that He has written on our lives. And it is through His power, that we may have and know more and more of God in our lives and stories.*

# INTRODUCTION

**The power of the resurrection**

The Power of the Resurrection is the focus of this Bible study. It is by God's power that we come to know Him as our Savior, and it is also by His power, the power of the resurrection, that we live our salvation out and know Him in our lives. As the Lord creates in us a desire to be students of His word, we may ONLY by His power be students of His word and also be able to know Him more and more through the word. The Lord, through the power of the resurrection, gives us the ability to be taught and to be reminded of who He is. Through the study of His word, the Holy Spirit guides us into His truth. Without Him and the power of the resurrection, we would not be able to live life in Him as He designed it. He is the author of our lives and stories. Who better than He, the power of the resurrection, to lead and guide us through?

With this as our focus, we will look at each Biblical person in this study through the lens of who God is in their story and what God does to enable each one on their journey. After all, it is all about Him, the Lord of the universe, who loved us so much that He was willing to die for us to live with Him. And thus, He sent His Holy Spirit to live in us, His presence to lead and to guide us today and forever. The Holy Spirit, power of the resurrection, has always been; He shows up in a myriad of ways to the people of the Old Testament and then in Jesus, of course, in the New.

We will take a look at the stories and lives of people in the Bible and at our own through who God is and who He says that He is, the power of the resurrection. Let's take a look at how we are going to do this study.

God gives us His word, His love letter, for us to know Him. To recap again, by the power of the Holy Spirit, the power of the resurrection, not only does He give us the desire to know Him, but He also gives us the capacity to know Him. Through His word, He teaches us who He is and what He does, and in addition, He reminds us again in the stories of His people. It took many iterations to hear what God wanted in this study of twelve men and women of the Old Testament and the New. I finally heard Him: it was to look for who He is in the story of His people. Aren't we seeking the One who created all? Isn't He whom we seek? God shares with us on the journey of our lives who He is. He comes to us and guides us into His hope, His story, the greatest of all stories.

The format evolved from describing the life and story to addressing the main question of who God is and what He does in the lives and stories of His children, thus, the power of the resurrection in the lives of those who believe Him and follow Him. The yearning each of us has is tied perfectly to who He is. He is the only One to fill and satisfy our deepest longings. And it is He who has the great story and plan for all, and above all, it is for His glory that we have the privilege of His great story and ours within it. Thus, the format focuses on the attributes of God as depicted in the lives and stories of His children. Who does He say that He is? And what does He say He does? It goes without saying that God's word is sufficient in its descriptions. This study gives attention to the character traits of God as depicted in His children's stories and how He is the counterpart to each need His children have in their lives and stories.

He is the same yesterday, today, and forever. The question then for the reader: "Are we going to by the power of the resurrection within us, given to us when we gave our lives to Jesus, lean into and trust our great God with our lives and lean into who He says He is for our every need?" If so, we may be taught and led into the knowledge of Him and also enabled, all by His power, to trust Him with our lives and stories.

**A personal study of twelve Biblical ancestors**

As we read God's word, He shows us Himself. He reveals who He is, His character, covenant, promises, and ways. We cannot do it on our own; only God through Jesus Christ reveals Himself through His word. We are not capable of knowing God unless He shows us the way. God teaches us, He reminds us, He gives us more and more of Himself in His word through the Holy Spirit, the power of the resurrection. During the last few years as I studied our ancestors of the Bible, God taught and reminded me of who He is in their lives and stories. The questions I generally would ask about a person in scripture became narrowed down to one. Who is He in this person's life? Who is God in my life, at this moment, during this pain or struggle, or as only He provides His comfort and peace?

God's ways are mystery. We cannot know everything about God or the ways of God. There are so many things we do not understand about the lives of persons in the Bible, nor will we, just as we will not understand our own or of those around us. However, God's word is His word to us. So often, we make His word about ourselves or about the people and how they lived or acted or failed or succeeded; yet, it is about God. God's perspective as He gives it to His children, the capacity or the mind to read and apply the scripture, is the means by which we study His word. As He taught me how to study His word, He helped me to know Him better. My prayer for this study is that you will know Him better. Well into writing this study, God showed me again one of my favorite scriptures, which He used to guide me over the last few years in my previous books, a fresh revelation to me again. Ephesians 1: 18-19 says:

> *"I pray that the eyes of your heart may be enlightened in order that you may know the hope to which he has called you, the riches of his glorious inheritance in his holy people, and his incomparably great power for us who believe. That power is the same as the mighty strength he exerted when he raised Christ from the dead and seated him at his right hand in the heavenly realms..."*

*Real Struggles, Real Hope: The Journey to Truth, Trust, and Freedom* (Westbow Press, 2013) describes the Hope to which God has called each one of us. Through the lens of His hope, I share how He was present from my early years into adulthood and what He taught me through His word about who He is and what He has done for all of us. Most importantly, the book highlights the great love story of God for us, the author of Hope in the midst of struggle indeed! The continuation of the story in *God Calls Us Daughters Extravagantly Loved* (Gibson, Johnson & Company, Inc., 2019) shows the depth of God's grace through Jesus Christ in adopting us as His children into relationship with Him as His Holy people. According to His plan all along, God's children live by the great power of the resurrection, the same the Lord exerted in raising Jesus from the dead, thus the third book, *More of God in Our Lives and Stories: The Power of the Resurrection*. Perhaps the most wonderful of all has been to study and write about who

He is from the perspective of the lives of God's children, who have gone before us by the power of the resurrection; they lived out the stories the Lord authored for each of them before the creation of the world. As we seek to know Him and ask who He is and what He does in the lives of His children, the biblical persons, and yes, ours, we know our Great God more and more.

**Who is He?**
"Who is this great God" becomes our question, which is the main theme of the Bible. Moses tells the Israelites that God is their life (Deuteronomy 30:19-20). Jesus says to seek Him above all (Matthew 7:7). And then in John 14:6, Jesus says that He is the way, the truth, and the life.

The overarching main story throughout scripture is God's love for His people through His Son, Jesus Christ. God is holy, yet accessible (Isaiah 57:15). He chooses relationship with us just as He did with Abraham when He made the covenant and with Moses when He gave him leadership of His people. God reveals Himself through the law and the prophets and then Jesus. He gives us all of Himself in Jesus Christ. The mystery is revealed through the glory of Jesus Christ.

God's people too have their stories but none are as wonderful as His. Yet, each one reflects the glory of the One and Only Savior by whom His children are able to live out their stories on this earth through eternity, to have the power to endure, to tell others about Him, and to go the journey with the knowledge of Him who was, who is, and who is to come.

God's glory in our stories is the thing we want to behold because it is God whom we yearn for, we seek, and who fills us with Himself in every way. Let us begin with "who is He?" It is the story worth living, the one for which we were made by the One who loves us without limit and whose glory we want to know.

**The importance of using the truths God reveals to us**
As we study the truths of God as demonstrated in His word, we want to reflect upon them and what they mean in our own stories and lives. Let's take a look at the themes in our own lives as we read the stories of our ancestors in the faith and study the themes in theirs.

We will see God showing up in their lives and intervening in moments of hardship but also at times one cannot explain. But God! As we pray and study, may we know what the Holy Spirit, the power of the resurrection, reveals to us about who God is in our own lives. Has His presence been more real at times? Do we know His comfort and rest in our difficulties? Or might we wonder from time to time where He is? His word as the Holy Spirit guides us will show us His heart for us. We can rest that He is who He says He is and does what He says He will do. We see it over and over again in scripture. May we know that it is true for our own lives too.

In this study, it is important to keep track of the truths the Lord is teaching you. At the end of each week, there is a reflection day and space for keeping track of your insights into the truths of God as they apply to your own life and story. May it be a gift to keep track of these truths each week and at the end of the study see all that the Lord has shown you about Him in your own life and story.

# DAILY FORMAT

HOW TO WORK THROUGH YOUR BIBLE STUDY

The invitation to you each day is to pray for God's leading as you read His word; as you pray, you may use the scripture outlined in the box for encouragement. Read the assigned scripture(s) and reflect on the questions for that day. Please note that the scripture reading for each day is essential for this study. As you read the scripture, ask the Holy Spirit to guide you in God's word; He will teach you new things, which you do not know. It is a privilege to study His word and to do it with you. I look forward to the insights and the transformations He makes in each of our lives as we delve into His word. To know Him more and more is my prayer for each one of us as we listen and allow Him to guide and teach us in His word, His love letter to us.

### Day One
*Who is God? Who is He in these scripture passages? How does God show His presence?*

### Day Two
*What is the dilemma? What is the problem for this Biblical person or persons in these scripture passages?*

### Day Three
*What is God's rescue? How does God show His care? What does God do to provide for this Biblical person or persons in these scripture passages?*

### Day Four
*What is the result of God's rescue? What happens in the scripture passages as a result of God's working (His rescue) or God's provision? What is the response to His provision?*

### Day Five
*What is God's story for His glory? How is God portrayed in this story? What does God give His people? How does the story reflect who God is?*

### Day Six
*What are the truths you have learned about God from this person's story? From your own story?*

### Perspectives

At the end of each chapter, there will be a perspective piece. These individual summaries together form a continuing perspective on the study of the lives of people, who are on the path of faith. They are in order but not related specifically to a particular Biblical person although each segment does appear between the chapters of the Bible study. You may read them together as a whole or as one of the larger context. Called a perspective piece, each one introduces an element on the journey of faith with our Father God, Lord and Rescuer, Jesus Christ, the Power of the Resurrection.

# OVERVIEW

WHO IS GOD?

Our great God has more in mind for us than all creation speaks. As we come to know Him more and more, our lives become more and more as He imagined for us, greater than we are able to fathom. We will never get to the end of God as He shares Himself with us through His Son, Jesus, and the Holy Spirit in this life and forever. Studying His word with the Holy Spirit's guidance, we come to know Him in new ways as He shows us who He is through others' lives as well as our own. His word illuminates our situations, good and bad, because He reveals what He has for us in His word. As we read and allow Him to guide us, He opens up the scriptures to what He has to teach us about Himself.

It is easier sometimes to see God working in another person's life than to see Him in our own. We cannot know another's feelings or even fully know their wants and needs, but we know that God loves and cares for each detail in their lives just as He does in ours. God recognizes our deep desires and our struggles before we know them. He knows our cries before we call.

As we study the lives and stories of God's children in the Old Testament and the New, God teaches us about who He is and what He does in the lives of His own. Our twelve include six men and six women. At the end of each of their chapters is a perspective piece on the journey of faith with our Father God, Lord and Rescuer, Jesus Christ, the Power of the Resurrection; they are interspersed throughout the study, not tied to a specific character.

This next space is just for you personally. Write a few statements/truths about God as you know Him. It could be statements that you know *about* Him. You may also want to write what you hope to find in this study that will be beneficial in your seeking God.

Introduction

PART I

# PETER

IT'S ALL ABOUT JESUS

MORE OF GOD IN OUR LIVES AND STORIES

PRAISE BE TO THE GOD AND FATHER OF OUR LORD JESUS CHRIST! IN HIS GREAT MERCY HE HAS GIVEN US NEW BIRTH INTO A LIVING HOPE THROUGH THE RESURRECTION OF JESUS CHRIST FROM THE DEAD, AND INTO AN INHERITANCE THAT CAN NEVER PERISH, SPOIL OR FADE. THIS INHERITANCE IS KEPT IN HEAVEN FOR YOU, WHO THROUGH FAITH ARE SHIELDED BY GOD'S POWER UNTIL THE COMING OF THE SALVATION THAT IS READY TO BE REVEALED IN THE LAST TIME. IN ALL THIS YOU GREATLY REJOICE, THOUGH NOW FOR A LITTLE WHILE YOU MAY HAVE HAD TO SUFFER GRIEF IN ALL KINDS OF TRIALS.

THESE HAVE COME SO THAT THE PROVEN GENUINENESS OF YOUR FAITH—OF GREATER WORTH THAN GOLD, WHICH PERISHES EVEN THOUGH REFINED BY FIRE—MAY RESULT IN PRAISE, GLORY AND HONOR WHEN JESUS CHRIST IS REVEALED. THOUGH YOU HAVE NOT SEEN HIM, YOU LOVE HIM; AND EVEN THOUGH YOU DO NOT SEE HIM NOW, YOU BELIEVE IN HIM AND ARE FILLED WITH AN INEXPRESSIBLE AND GLORIOUS JOY, FOR YOU ARE RECEIVING THE END RESULT OF YOUR FAITH, THE SALVATION OF YOUR SOULS.

1 PETER 1:3-9

## PART I

# PETER

#### IT'S ALL ABOUT JESUS

It is fitting to start our study with Peter. He was the one Jesus chose to lead the church after the resurrection. Indeed, He told Peter to wait until they had received the promised Holy Spirit to go out and spread the gospel. At Pentecost, Peter, filled with the Holy Spirit as were all the people in the temple, gave the sermon of his life. They experienced the power of the resurrection firsthand. The mystery unfolded, at least in part, that day.

As it was with Peter, each person who answers the call to follow Jesus and chooses to follow Jesus, is given the power to do so by the Holy Spirit. It is by the power of the resurrection that the church was built on the foundation of Jesus and the working of the Holy Spirit in believers' hearts. Each of us has been given this power with the indwelling of the Holy Spirit when we make the step of faith. We have been given the capacity to know our Father God through the Son, Jesus Christ.

✦

**Mystery**
Jesus comes into the life of Peter and shows him who He is.
Have you had an encounter with Him? Peter's story shows us who God is,
and as we study it in scripture, the Lord instructs us in His ways.

**Power**
Becoming a fisher of men, receiving the filling at Pentecost, and becoming a
leader in the early church—all were enabled by the power of the resurrection.
Where have you experienced God's power?

**Paradox**
A real fisherman became a fisher of men; it was God's plan.
What is God's plan in your life?

# PETER

DAY ONE - WHO IS GOD?

*Jesus always shows up*

Today has begun like any other with morning routine and then work. All seems pretty mundane. Casting nets into the water and hoping for a great catch, yet feeling the weight of the daily work, I welcome a passerby, someone I have never seen. Jesus approaches and says, "Follow me," and I do. This is the story of Peter. Where are you on this day which doesn't seem out of the ordinary at all. What hopes are tucked way down deep? Are you pulled down by the dailyness of your life?

This day forever changed Peter's life! God chose Peter. He has chosen you too. Do you know that? Jesus actually walked up to Peter, and He still comes to us. He intervenes in the dailyness of life. He always shows up! Are we ready to follow? Peter may have surprised himself by doing so. Jesus said, "I will make you a fisher of men." Peter must have thought it a mysterious promise.

It is true of us too who follow Jesus. It is mystery. God changes us as we take a step in His direction, as we follow in His footsteps. Just as Peter did, we go after the One who calls us to follow. We don't know exactly where, but the who, Jesus, is in front of us. Deep within, we know it is whom we want to know.

✦

**Author's note**
*The box below includes scripture to encourage you as you read and study God's word*

> "I PRAY THAT THE EYES OF YOUR HEART MAY BE ENLIGHTENED IN ORDER THAT YOU MAY KNOW THE HOPE TO WHICH HE HAS CALLED YOU, THE RICHES OF HIS GLORIOUS INHERITANCE IN HIS HOLY PEOPLE, AND HIS INCOMPARABLY GREAT POWER FOR US WHO BELIEVE. THAT POWER IS THE SAME AS THE MIGHTY STRENGTH HE EXERTED WHEN HE RAISED CHRIST FROM THE DEAD AND SEATED HIM AT HIS RIGHT HAND IN THE HEAVENLY REALMS..." - EPHESIANS 1:18-20

**Read Matthew 4 and Acts 2**
What do these scripture passages teach us about who God is? Other ways to ask and answer the question: How does God show up? How does God show His presence? Write your answers on the following page.

# PETER

DAY ONE - WHO IS GOD?

# PETER

DAY TWO - WHAT IS THE DILEMMA?

*Jesus meets us where we are (grace abounds)*

Day after day, Peter saw Jesus performing miracles, healing the sick, feeding thousands, casting out demons, teaching, and providing. We too witness firsthand the provision of God daily. God comes. God provides. He meets us where we are: sick in sin, downtrodden, or without hope of a cure. We do not rise to meet Him; Jesus comes down to us. Grace is the answer, and He provides. Peter witnessed Jesus' many acts of grace. Are you aware? Have you awakened to the grace of each breath, the sunrise, and a day filled with its own promise when delivered by Jesus?

As Peter followed Jesus from crowd to crowd teaching and healing, he saw things he had never imagined. What would our thoughts have been if He healed our mother-in-law, or made the paralyzed walk, or healed a woman by casting her demons into the sea? His teaching like that of a rabbi, but so much more, confronted, rebuked, and yet ministered in its truth, righteousness, and justice. Might we have been offended or doubted its veracity? Or could we have been awestruck, humbled, and saved by the grace of our Savior Jesus? How is it going today? What provision or grace is being extended to you today? How is your heart? Open to new, ready for grace? Or closed off, fearful of more, skeptical, or apathetic that healing and miracles exist? Perhaps it's your heart showing its need for the grace right in front of you!

✦

> "I BECAME A SERVANT OF THE GOSPEL BY THE GIFT OF GOD'S GRACE GIVEN ME BY THE WORKING OF HIS POWER." - EPHESIANS 3:7

**Read Mark chapters 5 through 9:**
The second segment introduces the second question: What is the dilemma?
In Peter's life, what does he face from day to day as he walks with Jesus? What are the problems Peter faces here? What are the issues addressed in this scripture passage?

# PETER

DAY TWO - WHAT IS THE DILEMMA?

# PETER

DAY THREE - WHAT IS GOD'S RESCUE?

*Jesus doesn't leave us where we are; Jesus turns things upside down*

God doesn't leave us where we are. He loves and pursues us. We are changed. We know we need Him (and the power of the Holy Spirit).

Peter continues to observe Jesus with the sick, lame, and demon-possessed and to hear Him teach and admonish the teachers of his day. Things were indeed upside down. Peter's beliefs were too. Where do we stand? Do we believe what Jesus taught?

Peter watched Jesus walk on water during a storm and received from Him the ability to do so too. He answered Jesus later when Jesus asked him, "Who do you say I am?" with "You are the Messiah, the Son of the living God." Jesus responds that only His Father in heaven reveals this knowledge. Yet, Peter made impetuous decisions and tried to circumvent Jesus' message and actions out of his own misguided interpretations. Jesus spoke of His suffering and death and even Peter's denial of Jesus. Peter's humanity overrode his ability to discern as did his perspective on who Jesus was as the Messiah and what that would mean. Sacrifice and suffering are not held in high esteem in the world of Peter's day or ours. Through the eyes of the world and Peter, Jesus needed to be protected from danger. What danger are you in? What dilemma is facing you: disease or physical suffering, a relationship betrayal, a difficult job or no work in sight, an addiction no one knows about, or a secret shame which keeps you from living to name a few?

We, like Peter, misunderstand Jesus. He comes to meet us where we are and He does not leave us there. Crazy world views, lies of the evil one, nothing is too hard for Him. He reveals Himself to us. And when He does, everything changes.

✦

> "I PRAY OUT OF HIS GLORIOUS RICHES HE MAY STRENGTHEN YOU
> WITH POWER THROUGH HIS SPIRIT IN YOUR INNER BEING..." - EPHESIANS 3:16

**Read Matthew 14:22-32; Matthew 16:13-18; Matthew 16:21-28**
In the third segment, what is God's rescue? What is God's provision for Peter? How does God rescue him? How does God show His care for Peter, for us? What does God do in the passage?

# PETER

DAY THREE - WHAT IS GOD'S RESCUE?

# PETER

DAY FOUR - WHAT IS THE RESULT OF GOD'S RESCUE?

*Jesus meets us in the trial and suffering to give us new life*

God chose Peter to walk along with Him, to see His sacrifice and suffering, and to know the real Messiah, not the one that Peter thought He would be, but the One God ordained in Jesus Christ. The Divine in human flesh came to live in persecution and die by crucifixion a criminal's death to serve the needy and to save the lost. A close friend and eyewitness, but bystander on so many levels, Peter denied knowing Jesus when things got dicey and then observed all that followed with Jesus' arrest, trial, and death on a cross. Yet, Jesus called Peter to be his disciple, the one upon whom He would depend to sacrifice, suffer, and serve just as He did.

Jesus shows up in our lives as He did Peter's and extends to us an invitation to walk with Him. Are we willing? Are we ready? To walk with Jesus, we will suffer. He met us when we were still sinners, and He continues to meet us to give us what we need in Him. Needing Him becomes what we know.

Peter met the women who saw Jesus' empty tomb. Still undone from Jesus' horrific death, Peter went to meet Him, their resurrected Savior and Lord. Can you imagine living as a disciple of Jesus as He was being sought after and killed and then three days later as He is alive and meeting you again? Suffering and sacrifice and life anew. Who is this Jesus?

Jesus is Peter's story. Peter would serve Jesus as proclaimer of the gospel message and in doing so would suffer violence and persecution. Jesus became who He said He was to Peter. Who is He becoming to you?

---

> "(YOU) MAY HAVE POWER, TOGETHER WITH ALL THE LORD'S HOLY PEOPLE, TO GRASP HOW WIDE AND LONG AND HIGH AND DEEP IS THE LOVE OF CHRIST AND TO KNOW THAT THIS LOVE SURPASSES KNOWLEDGE THAT YOU MAY BE FILLED TO THE MEASURE OF ALL THE FULLNESS OF GOD." - EPHESIANS 3:18-19

**Read Matthew 26-28**

In the fourth segment, what is the result of God's rescue? What happens in Peter's life? Describe the result of the ultimate rescue of God during these passages of scripture for Peter and for all of us.

# PETER

DAY FOUR - WHAT IS THE RESULT OF GOD'S RESCUE?

The Power of The Resurrection in Peter's Life

# PETER

DAY FIVE - WHAT IS "THE STORY FOR GOD'S GLORY?"

*Jesus is the new life, the story to be told; He turns our lives inside out to worship and praise Him*

God reveals Himself as He did in Jesus. Jesus show us who He is, willing to suffer, even die for us. Walking in His footsteps became the means by which Peter knew his Lord. There is no other way. In the trial of betraying Jesus, in the impetuous judgements and actions, in the anxiety and fear, and in the misguided notions of who a Messiah is, God in Jesus taught his disciple how to know and love Him, to stand strong, to serve, and to love with the heart of God to the glory of God.

Jesus had told his disciples to wait before they began their mission of spreading the good news of Jesus to the world, to wait for the power of the Holy Spirit. At Pentecost, Peter filled with the Spirit of the Lord, spoke with authority and power. With the Holy Spirit's indwelling, the disciples were ready to spread the gospel. The church, in its infancy empowered by the news of Jesus Christ, began.
What work has God established in you? Are you leaning on Him empowered by His Holy Spirit? Peter late in his life continued the good work in writing two letters of the New Testament. Inspired to teach truth, to encourage the scattered and persecuted believers, and to exhort them to discern false teaching, Peter was still living out Jesus' story in his life. Is Jesus your story? He is waiting to be.

✦

> "FINALLY, BE STRONG IN THE LORD AND IN HIS MIGHTY POWER." - EPHESIANS 6:10:

### Read Acts 2 and 1st and 2nd Peter

What is "the story for God's glory?" What changes in Peter's life demonstrate what the Lord has done for Peter? How does Peter praise God for who He is, and how does Peter thank Him for what He has done?

# PETER

DAY FIVE - WHAT IS "THE STORY FOR GOD'S GLORY?"

# PETER

DAY SIX - WHAT ARE GOD'S TRUTHS?

*Trusting God through our own failure*

Why am I afraid of failure? Not pleasing others; letting others down, causing hurt? All is about Jesus. His truth and grace cover all. Pride is a cover for self-importance. Getting it right is also a cover, a self-protection. Instead of it being a virtue, it is a sin, one that is full of hiding and running from the One who provides what is right and good and rescue from all else. Jesus covers all the sin and shameful places in our souls. He takes our brokenness and does something with it for His purposes.

Peter was impulsive and protective of Jesus who did not need protecting; Jesus was the protector. Am I trying to protect myself from failing? Am I afraid of causing hurt? Am I afraid of being blamed? All of these come from a place of woundedness; no amount of caution keeps one from failing, hurting, or hurting others. Jesus is the counterpart of failure and hurt. He addresses the wound with His truth and grace; only He makes one healed and whole. Walking in the trenches of the broken places of failure and disappointing the ones you love the most, if one allows Him, Jesus steps in and gives grace. His grace heals, protects, provides, comforts, and becomes the conduit for change right where the brokenness began and resides.

Peter knew all about disappointing Jesus and himself. He knew all about failure. His failure to acknowledge Jesus was not only a pivotal moment in the life of Peter but also one for each of us as we read the scripture. It represents each of us. Jesus still built the church on the foundation just as He came to do, and He chose Peter as the first disciple. Jesus doesn't call us to come to Him after we have gotten better; He comes to us where we are, the sinful and broken, who need Him desperately.
As we turn our lives toward Him, He turns us inside out as we come to know that it is all about Jesus.

✦

> "BUT WHEN HE, THE SPIRIT OF TRUTH, COMES, HE WILL GUIDE YOU INTO ALL THE TRUTH."
> - JOHN 16:13A

### *Reflections*
*Reflect on the truths of God you have learned in Peter's life. And your own? One truth from Peter's life for reflection may be to ask: How does God enable Peter to trust Him in his failure? Other truths upon which to reflect that may present a paradox to us: Why would Jesus choose Peter as the one to preach to the early church? Why does He choose us?*

# PETER

DAY SIX - WHAT ARE GOD'S TRUTHS?

# A PERSPECTIVE
### THE SEARCH FOR MORE—ASKING FOR MORE OF GOD IN OUR STORIES

In our day, we are we seeking more time with our families and friends, more joy in our lives, more recreation and time away from responsibility, more peace, more what? How do we even go after these things we ponder? Has our search just begun or is it the same old question from yesterday or last year? Perhaps we know deep within that who we are and what we are doing is not satisfactory. We could be seekers of God or believers of God or perhaps neither. My conclusion is that we all are seeking the God who created us and for whom we are wired. If you have not chosen to seek God in Jesus Christ, now is the time. And if you are a believer in Jesus Christ as I am, you may still be going after many good things, and all the while you may not have set your heart upon the one for which God is pursuing in you. *What if we wanted more of God in our lives? What if we asked for more of God in our lives and stories?*

We have a choice to allow God into our lives. When we choose, God gives us the capacity to invite Him in; this empowerment to do so is faith. God gives us faith. Faith is the assurance of things hoped for and the certainty of things unseen. By faith we have God in our lives and stories.

God's love has been poured into our hearts through the Holy Spirit (Romans 5:1-5). He empowers us to persevere through the hard times and suffering and to have hope that all is not lost but that we have life in Him forever. Hope in Christ is what we seek during the difficult times. By faith we become strong in our hope in Him and know the love of Christ given to us through the fellowship of His Holy Spirit and others who believe in Him.

It is also by faith that we collaborate with God in our lives through joy and pain. When we go through the hard things and we allow God to show us the way and guide us through them, He becomes our story. He is ours. By faith we know the God of the universe in Jesus Christ. By faith, "Who is He?" becomes our question as we seek to know Him and know Him more. He is our glorious Father, the God of our Lord Jesus Christ. By faith given in a Spirit of wisdom and revelation to know Him better, we know the hope to which He has called us; we know the riches of the inheritance of His holy people; and we know the incomparably great power, the power of the resurrection (Ephesians 1:17-20).

We grasp His love for us, for all of God's people. Through their witness, we know Him better; we know His love more. It is through their lives and stories we know the love of Christ. By faith our common bond with others through the Holy Spirit empowers us to hear and know Him better. As we stand with others in their lives and hear their stories of His power, we know the power that makes it possible for us to make it through the hard times and for Him to be known to the world through them. God gives us the privilege to suffer in His name and to tell others about Him.

We fix our focus on Jesus to persevere in this journey on this earth. His power gives us the perseverance to go the depth and the length of it. Reminded that He loved us enough to die the cruel death He did in the midst of being treated more savagely than we can imagine, by faith we know that He did it for you and for me (Hebrews 12:1-2). Jesus becomes by faith our advocate, guide, and counselor on this life journey. He goes before us, with us, and after us. By faith He, the greater story, becomes our story.

Diving into the lives of some of God's children in the Bible, by faith we will know Him better through asking, "Who is He?" in their stories. What does God reveal about Himself? Their stories give us a glimpse of our Lord Jesus Christ in real life. Who is He in your real life? Do you want to know Him more? Do you want more of Him in your life and story? He is waiting to show you more of Himself. He stands at the door and knocks. He says to ask, seek, and find Him. Are we willing to step out in faith and ask Him for more?

God gave each of these characters more of Himself. Most of them were unlikely beneficiaries of this truth just as all of us are. We are undeserving and empty and full of ourselves and what the world offers us until by faith we let go and let God. In the midst of the story, He gives us more and more of Himself, and we are transformed by Him. Truly it is the power of God in the life of His children. What are we waiting for? Let's hear what God has to say about who He is and what He does in the lives of His children. In addition, may we learn and know what God cares about in our lives and stories. What is the most important thing on God's heart? Might we consider that as we are as unlikely as each character we are reading about, that God just may be doing something like it in our own lives and stories? And might we be willing to ask Him to be our story, the main character, the more for which we have been seeking?

✦

Is asking God for more of Him in your life a genuine request for you right now? If so, would you ask Him? If not, why not?

How do you spend time with God? Does it include seeking Him for a better relationship with Him?

What are your questions for God? How might you increase your seeking Him?

When you go to God in prayer, does it feel like an obligation or a relationship? How would you change your prayer life?

When do you go to God?

PART II

# ABRAHAM

GOD'S WAY

MORE OF GOD IN OUR LIVES AND STORIES

BY FAITH ABRAHAM, WHEN CALLED TO GO TO A PLACE HE WOULD LATER RECEIVE AS HIS INHERITANCE, OBEYED AND WENT, EVEN THOUGH HE DID NOT KNOW WHERE HE WAS GOING. BY FAITH HE MADE HIS HOME IN THE PROMISED LAND LIKE A STRANGER IN A FOREIGN COUNTRY; HE LIVED IN TENTS, AS DID ISAAC AND JACOB, WHO WERE HEIRS WITH HIM OF THE SAME PROMISE.

HEBREWS 11: 8-9

# PART II
# ABRAHAM
GOD'S WAY

Let's switch back to the Old Testament where we see God showing up in Abraham's life to start a nation of His people through Abraham, who was old and with his wife had not been able to conceive a child. This plan was as it had always been. God knew when He created Abraham that He had chosen Him to be a father of many descendants. And through them, the world would know Him.

Abraham heard God and followed Him by the power of God, yes, the power of the resurrection, even though it had not occurred yet. God's power is the only way a human being can turn from his own way and choose to follow God. When Abraham chose to believe and follow God, God gave him the faith to continue and move his entire family to a place he did not know. God calls us into this faith, and He also names us His own when we turn around to go with Him.

✦

**Mystery**
God calls us His own.

**Power**
Abraham heard God and followed Him.

**Paradox**
It does not matter that Abraham and Sarah could not conceive.
God chose them to have many descendants; nothing is too big for Him.

# ABRAHAM

DAY ONE - WHO IS GOD?

*God calls us*

Do you recall that God shows up? God calls Abraham. What does this really mean? God chooses to pursue His children and to call them His own. God speaks to Abraham with a command and a promise. Let us delve a little deeper. First, God chooses with whom He speaks; after all, He is God Almighty, the Lord of the universe. In addition, He chooses to speak to them. Abraham was listening. Are we? Not only does He speak to Abraham, but He also gives guidance and He gives assurances about that which He is speaking. God reveals Himself in ways that we know that it is He. It is strong and convicting, and yet it is also familiar and intimate; Abraham must have known this too.

Abraham did as God commanded. He went in the direction God called him, and he did so without knowing what the future held. God called Abraham "righteous" because he followed after God without knowing where he was going. Do we know where we are going? Are we willing to follow God without knowing where we are going?

As Abraham obeyed, meaning that he followed what God had commanded, God gave Him the assurance along the way and encouraged him in the way he was following after God. Abraham worshipped and gave thanks to God; he acknowledged that God was leading the way and providing for him as he went. God led Abraham with each step he took in the direction God had given him.

Isn't this the way God works? He gives us the next step. In Abraham's case, God told him to leave his country and go in the direction of Canaan. Abraham obeyed God, and God blessed him. With each new step, God gave Abraham more and more assurance of the many blessings that were in store for him and his descendants. God speaks to us and gives us the ability to follow Him. As we follow Him, He assures us of His provision along the way. God makes good on His promises always.

✦

> "I PRAY THAT THE EYES OF YOUR HEART MAY BE ENLIGHTENED IN ORDER THAT YOU MAY KNOW THE HOPE TO WHICH HE HAS CALLED YOU, THE RICHES OF HIS GLORIOUS INHERITANCE IN HIS HOLY PEOPLE AND HIS INCOMPARABLY GREAT POWER FOR US WHO BELIEVE. THAT POWER IS THE SAME AS THE MIGHTY STRENGTH HE EXERTED WHEN HE RAISED CHRIST FROM THE DEAD AND SEATED HIM AT HIS RIGHT HAND IN THE HEAVENLY REALMS." - EPHESIANS 1:18-20

**Read Genesis 12; John 10:3; Romans 4**
In this first segment, who is God? How does He present Himself to Abraham?

# ABRAHAM

DAY ONE - WHO IS GOD?

# ABRAHAM

DAY TWO - WHAT IS THE DILEMMA?

*God fulfills His promises despite our sin*

God knows our every thought, desire, and movement. He knows our sin and loves us still. He demonstrates this truth by sacrificing His only Son for us to be in relationship with Him. God does not leave us in our own mess; He comes to rescue us through His Son, Jesus. God shows us who He is. Despite who we are, God loves us still.

God knows Abraham's heart to follow Him, and God also knows that Abraham has faults and will falter from the path of following after Him. When God shows Abraham the way to Canaan, He knows beforehand the ways He will need to rescue Abraham. God is not surprised by our choices. Where has God needed to rescue you? Have you received His rescue? God doesn't change who He is. When we decide to follow Him, He sees us as He sees Jesus, His only son. Before we make the decision to follow Him, He pursues us in our sin to follow Him. As His children, He promises to be with us and never to forsake us. He fulfills His promises.

Abraham feared Pharaoh and asked his wife, Sarah, to pretend to be his sister so that Pharaoh would extend favor to them. Sarah did as Abraham asked, and it was a harrowing experience to be in Pharaoh's presence as Abraham's sister instead of his wife. God still honored His promises to Abraham even though Abraham did not trust God and acted out of fear and anxiety. God does not treat His children as we deserve but as the Father God He is, good, gracious, compassionate, slow to anger, and faithful. When have you acted out of fear and anxiety? Do you know that you can trust your Father God who has good plans for you as His child? He loves you in spite of your mess ups, fear, or not following Him. God's way is that we turn our hearts toward Him, that we come to Him, and that we know Him and love Him. He knows our hearts as He did Abraham's, and He helps us to go His way.

---

> "I BECAME A SERVANT OF THE GOSPEL BY THE GIFT OF GOD'S GRACE GIVEN ME BY THE WORKING OF HIS POWER." - EPHESIANS 3:7

### Read Genesis 13-14; Psalm 145

In this second segment, what is the dilemma for Abraham and Sarah? What are the problems they face?

# ABRAHAM

DAY TWO - WHAT IS THE DILEMMA?

# ABRAHAM

DAY THREE - WHAT IS GOD'S RESCUE?

*God provides in ways beyond our imagination*

Abraham and his wife, Sarah, were close to a hundred years old; their days of child-bearing were long gone, so they thought. When God told Abraham he would have many descendants and that the world would be blessed through them, he could not imagine how that could be, but he still followed God's commands. Sarah had doubts. She arranged for a concubine, Hagar, to have Abraham's child that they would call their own. Her eagerness to make things work out the way she wanted them got in the way. Yet, God blessed them with a son, Ishmael, through Hagar, Abraham's concubine. Have you even taken matters in your own hands when things were not moving fast enough for you? It is difficult to wait and so easy to jump ahead of God, but He works in His own time, which is ultimately for our good.

Abraham and Sarah were also blessed to birth a son, Isaac, in their old age just as God had told them. It seemed so improbable, but with God all things are possible. What looks improbable in your life or even impossible?

God provides in ways that are beyond our imagination. His ways are not our own. He loves us and pursues us with His outstretched arm. God has plans for us that are good and that are full of hope. Perhaps you have placed your hope in something other than God? Could God be giving you time to cry out to Him? He is interested in you and your heart just as He was interested in Abraham and Sarah's hearts. His promise to them was to bless them and through them to bless the nations. God's dreams for us are so much bigger than we ask or imagine (Ephesians 3:20-21). He is the creator of great wonders and miracles. His lovingkindness toward us, His children, is greater than we know. Are we ready to experience the wonder of His great love?

✦

> "I PRAY OUT OF HIS GLORIOUS RICHES HE MAY STRENGTHEN YOU WITH POWER THROUGH HIS SPIRIT IN YOUR INNER BEING..." - EPHESIANS 3:16

**Read Genesis 15-20; Ephesians 3:20-21**
In this third segment, what is God's rescue? How does He provide for Abraham and Sarah? What does God do in this scripture passage? How does God show His care for them?

# ABRAHAM

DAY THREE - WHAT IS GOD'S RESCUE?

# ABRAHAM

DAY FOUR - WHAT IS THE RESULT OF GOD'S RESCUE?

*God, in His faithfulness, reveals Himself to us*

Who is this God who shows Abraham the wonder of His love by giving him a son in his old age and then says that he must take him up on the mount and sacrifice him? He is the same yesterday, today, and forever. He promises to provide, to stay with us, and never to leave us. Yet, in our nearsightedness, God may seem not so close at times only to show up to rescue us seemingly at the last minute. God shows up on the mount in a ram in the thicket; Abraham had just said to Isaac that God would provide a sacrifice, and He did. Again, the rescuer provides for His own.

Even in the story of Hagar, Abraham's concubine, and the son she had with Abraham, Ishmael, He provided. Trouble developed between Sarah and Hagar. God told Abraham to let them go, to allow Sarah to send them away. How could a good God send them away or ask a father to sacrifice a son? As life unfolds, God allows difficult things in our lives, but He does not leave us in them. He gives us Himself and provides for us even in the struggle and the hard times. Abraham trusted God with the gifts He had given Him.

Are you imagining what you are to do if you are "left high and dry?" In other words, are you coming up on your last and there does not seem to be a solution, an answer, a provision for the circumstance you are in? Are you too close? God sees the whole, inside out, and from a distance and close up. Have you asked Him to intervene? Abraham, given the ability to believe God by God, knew the Giver of all good things, God Himself. He did not doubt that God would provide. After, all, God promised He would. He made a covenant with Abraham to give him many descendants and bless them. God does not have in His character to lie or to fail at keeping a promise. God in His faithfulness gives us the capacity to trust Him just as He did Abraham. At the same time, God keeps on being faithful to His promises. Do you know God? As a promise keeper? As a provider? The Giver of all good things?

✦

> "(YOU) MAY HAVE POWER, TOGETHER WITH ALL THE LORD'S HOLY PEOPLE, TO GRASP HOW WIDE AND LONG AND HIGH AND DEEP IS THE LOVE OF CHRIST AND TO KNOW THAT THIS LOVE SURPASSES KNOWLEDGE THAT YOU MAY BE FILLED TO THE MEASURE OF ALL THE FULLNESS OF GOD." - EPHESIANS 3:18-19

**Read Genesis 21-22; Psalm 57**
In this fourth segment, what is the result of God's rescue?
How has God become more to Abraham in his life? What is Abraham's response to God?

# ABRAHAM

DAY FOUR - WHAT IS THE RESULT OF GOD'S RESCUE?

# ABRAHAM

DAY FIVE - WHAT IS THE "STORY FOR GOD'S GLORY?"

*God's faithfulness changes us*

Abraham's story is one like many others in God's word; God's faithfulness became his. God's heart changed Abraham from the inside out. He followed God and during the process came to know the One who sent him into a land he did not know and also kept providing in the most difficult times. Isn't this what being a follower of God is? God does the leading because He created us, loves us, and has a plan for us; He knows where we are going when we do not.

Abraham came to know the great God of the universe through trial and suffering. He left his home and followed God without knowing where he was going. He did not have children of his own in his later years. When God gave them to him, He also seemed to be taking them away, first, Ishmael, then Isaac. What would you think was going on if you were in Abraham's shoes?

As Abraham lived through the hard times, his trust became greater in the God he knew, the God who had led the way from his far away home to his new one. God's faithfulness never wavered. He is a God of promise and of fulfilling His promises. Knowing God became Abraham's life. He wanted to live this life and to pass it on to his descendants. He requested a servant to find a wife for Isaac, one of their own, God's children. The generations would be blessed by God, the God of promise. Standing in God's presence and sharing His blessings with His descendants, Abraham became the vessel of God's faithfulness. God's faithfulness became his.

Along the way to Canaan, Abraham stopped and worshipped God, raised monuments, and named them on his way to the land God promised him. God became a bigger and bigger part of Abraham's journey. Is God's faithfulness part of your story? How big a part?

✦

> "FINALLY, BE STRONG IN THE LORD AND IN HIS MIGHTY POWER." - EPHESIANS 6:10

**Read Genesis 24; Psalm 105**
What is the story for God's glory in Abraham's life? How is Abraham's life changed through God's rescue? How would you describe his gratitude and praise to the Lord?

# ABRAHAM

DAY FIVE - WHAT IS THE "STORY FOR GOD'S GLORY?"

# ABRAHAM

DAY SIX - WHAT ARE GOD'S TRUTHS?

*Trusting God when you have to leave all behind*

God gave Abraham the means to follow Him to Canaan. The faith to follow the Lord is a gift; yet, Abraham knew the way and got lost a few times with his wife, Sarah. Isn't it like that with us too? I still try to go my way with my plans for life, with my concerns for my family, with my days and hours; yet, I know the way, and He is Jesus. I lose my way just as Abraham. What causes us to lose our way? Sometimes we jump ahead of God. We want God to endorse our plan. Often, fear causes me to stumble; instead of trusting God, I turn to other things, including my own understanding. God says that we are to trust Him and He will direct our paths. Abraham trusted God, and God directed his path.

How am I doing trusting Him? Are His paths my paths? Am I following Him or asking Him to validate the path I'm on? It's simple, but perhaps not that easy. With direction, He also gives a way to follow it. In my life, I find that He gives me the capacity to do as He has directed; sometimes I have to wait for it.

✦

> "BUT WHEN HE, THE SPIRIT OF TRUTH, COMES, HE WILL GUIDE YOU INTO ALL THE TRUTH."
> - JOHN 16:13

### Reflections

Reflect on the truths of God you have learned in Abraham's life. And your own?
How does God enable Abraham to trust Him with leaving all he had behind?
What has "trusting God through leaving all that we know" from Abraham's
life taught you about God?

# ABRAHAM

DAY SIX - WHAT ARE GOD'S TRUTHS?

# A PERSPECTIVE

HARDSHIP AND THE POWER OF THE RESURRECTION

God provides when difficulty comes. What I know now that I haven't always known is that it is what ushers us into the place where we meet Him. It is often not in the way I expect; however, the Lord God in Jesus Christ shows me who He is. He is my father, protector, rescuer, counselor, guide; as Moses says in Deuteronomy, He is our life. We admit our need for Him, that we do not have the answers, and we cry out to Him. It is in leaning into Him and acknowledging the pain, the lack, the sin, the wound, or the broken place that provides the place where we meet Him, who knows exactly what we are going through. There is nothing that would keep Him from meeting us here.

This revelation for each child of God is the desire of God's heart. He knows that we need Him; He is pursuing us to pour out His love and grace on us. He is waiting to become the father He always has been. Our necessary suffering, if you will, is a place where our eyes, ears, or hearts may open. When this happens, we have found the spacious place God has wanted us to receive. God meets us wherever we are. He is not choosey. We cannot go where He does not. Does He want us to go to some of the places we go? No, but the One who is Holy meets us, sinners, in our places of greatest need. Jesus made it so!

Studying the power of the resurrection in the lives of God's children allows us to see how God reveals Himself to them and to us in suffering, pain, struggle, difficult and stressful times, the moments when we know that we do not have all that it takes to fix, move through, or endure our circumstances. Our disappointment, betrayal, death, or loss brings us to the end of ourselves. We need God. When we finally turn to Him, we meet Him. He has been here all along; we weren't ready. God in Jesus Christ brings light out of the darkness, new out of the old ways, and life out of death. God did it on resurrection day over 2000 years ago. He did it once and for all and for all of us, His children. He offers this same life to us. He has given it; we must tap into it.

Even as ones who profess to follow Jesus, we sometimes do not get it. The power is not there for us, we feel. His new life is not new enough or good enough. It does not seem better. Who are we following? Who is in the driver seat? When we give it up and allow Him in, He will provide more than we imagine. It is the place for which we have yearned in the midst of the hard times; He Himself is with us to love, guide, protect, and walk or carry us through. It is God Himself in Jesus Christ who reveals the power of the resurrection in our lives. He has come, and we have come to know Him in the suffering. This is the power of the resurrection; Jesus rose so that we may live. Living is Jesus Christ, and He is the life.

What our ancestors found as will we on this journey is that He is God and there is no other. We search high and low, we try this or that, and we come up empty except when we seek Him while He may be found.

*Why do we not talk of God's Power?* Is it because we do not rely upon Him for it? Or do we not believe that it exists? How then do we live with His Power? Fearful of His Power, halfheartedly embracing His Power, retreating from His Power, or leaning into and holding tight to God? God's power on earth and in heaven is the same God exerted in the power of Jesus' resurrection from the dead. His word in Ephesians 1:19 says that this power is the same as that which God exerted during the resurrection of Jesus. It is the way He wants us to live, by His Power. God's intention was to live and die for us, the ultimate sacrifice, in order for us to be at peace with Him and to live in relationship with Him on earth and for eternity. This power is God's grace to us in the gift of His Son, who is His own and the one for whom we will all bow in heaven and on earth. Not only did He give us the ultimate sacrifice, but He also gave us the means by which to be in relationship with Him through His Holy Spirit. The power is indescribable but authentic and real because of the person of Jesus Christ.

By God's power, He creates, saves, guides, teaches, reminds, and goes before, with, and behind us. He reveals His own nature through His Son who came to live and die for us, and then He rescues and delivers us to be His own with His own Spirit to dwell within to move, and live, and for us to be able to commune with and for Him. Throughout the Bible, God shows us His people and His intention for their lives. He demonstrates for us His promises and His power to fulfill them through the stories of His children. We, His children, also have His promises and plans, and He uses His power to show us Himself and our lives to show the world who He is. His purposes and plan will not be thwarted by anything or anyone; however, we, as part of His plan, may participate in the greatest story ever told, His story of His love and power, the gift of His Son, Jesus, to all.

His power is the only way for us. It becomes the mark of a child of God. We cannot deny the grace He has given, nor can we deprive Him of the power He displays within us when we become His children. We bear His name as children of God, the great I AM.

The power of God is a huge and divine intervention in our lives. Not only was it God's plan from the beginning, but it is His purpose for us as His children. The world will know Him by His power and revelation of Jesus Christ. He lives within and gives us the grace and power to stay close to Him and go out into the world to serve.

Where do you go when things get tough?

Have you experienced God in the hard things?

Would you ask God for help in letting go and letting Him help you in the difficulties you are facing right now?

PART III

# RAHAB

GOD'S CHOICE

MORE OF GOD IN OUR LIVES AND STORIES

BEFORE THE SPIES LAY DOWN FOR THE NIGHT, SHE WENT UP ON THE ROOF AND SAID TO THEM, "I KNOW THAT THE LORD HAS GIVEN YOU THIS LAND AND THAT A GREAT FEAR OF YOU HAS FALLEN ON US, SO THAT ALL WHO LIVE IN THIS COUNTRY ARE MELTING IN FEAR BECAUSE OF YOU. WE HAVE HEARD HOW THE LORD DRIED UP THE WATER OF THE RED SEA FOR YOU WHEN YOU CAME OUT OF EGYPT, AND WHAT YOU DID TO SIHON AND OG, THE TWO KINGS OF THE AMORITES EAST OF THE JORDAN, WHOM YOU COMPLETELY DESTROYED. WHEN WE HEARD OF IT, OUR HEARTS MELTED IN FEAR AND EVERYONE'S COURAGE FAILED BECAUSE OF YOU, FOR THE LORD YOUR GOD IS GOD IN HEAVEN ABOVE AND ON THE EARTH BELOW.

JOSHUA 2:8-11

PART III

# RAHAB
GOD'S CHOICE

God's ways are not our ways. He shows Himself to whom He chooses. Often, it is the most unlikely person God chooses for His purposes. In this case, He chooses Rahab, a prostitute, to help the Israelites defeat their enemies in Jericho and enter the long-awaited Promised Land.

Not only does He keep the covenant He made with His people generations ago, but He keeps the promises He makes to each of us personally. God is a promise giver and keeper. The story within the larger story here is that Rahab wants her family to be spared during this battle; not only does God deliver Jericho into the hands of Joshua and the Israelites, but He also saves Rahab and her family, who lived in Jericho's walls.

✦

**Mystery**
God's ways are not ours. Do you have something in your life
where God has shown up in a mysterious way.

**Power**
God fights the battles. He gives sight to those whose
hearts are turned toward Him.

**Paradox**
It is the least among us to whom God makes Himself known. The spies found
safety and protection, given by God through the prostitute, Rahab.

The Power of the Resurrection in Rahab's Life

# RAHAB

DAY ONE - WHO IS GOD?

*God's choosing gives us a choice to make*

When Joshua made plans to lead the Israelites into the Promised Land, he sent spies into the land to check it out. God shows up in Rahab's life as the spies ask her for help. Have you considered that God may send a person to you? Rahab took the spies seriously; she and her people had observed the neighboring regions and the battles among them. When the spies asked her to let them hide in the walls of Jericho in her home, she said "yes." Are you saying "yes" to God?

God chooses whom He wants to use for His purposes. He chooses to make you His child, and He gives you the opportunity to decide to follow Him. His choosing gives each of us a choice to make. Rahab, a prostitute, lived hidden in the walls of Jericho. She was known fully by God. He chose her as the means by which the Israelites would enter the Promised Land. What has God chosen you to do? God chooses whom He chooses, not as the world sees, not as the world chooses, and certainly not as the world proclaims. God chooses His own. God gives each of us a purpose as we live on this earth, one that He gave to us before creation and that will bring glory to His name.

God not only chose her but gave Rahab the ability to see and choose wisely. Rahab considered the spies as those who were supporting the cause of God. She saw them as His messengers. Choosing God's way enabled the promise of God to be fulfilled. Are you choosing God's way?

✦

> "I PRAY THAT THE EYES OF YOUR HEART MAY BE ENLIGHTENED IN ORDER THAT YOU MAY KNOW THE HOPE TO WHICH HE HAS CALLED YOU, THE RICHES OF HIS GLORIOUS INHERITANCE IN HIS HOLY PEOPLE, AND HIS INCOMPARABLY GREAT POWER FOR US WHO BELIEVE. THAT POWER IS THE SAME AS THE MIGHTY STRENGTH HE EXERTED WHEN HE RAISED CHRIST FROM THE DEAD AND SEATED HIM AT HIS RIGHT HAND IN THE HEAVENLY REALMS ..." - EPHESIANS 1:18-20

**Read Joshua 2; Matthew 1:5**
In this first segment, who is God? Who is He? How does God show up for Rahab in this scripture passage? How does God show up for the Israelites?

# RAHAB

DAY ONE - WHO IS GOD?

# RAHAB

DAY TWO - WHAT IS THE DILEMMA?

*God always provides for His own*

God's plan was already in place when Joshua sent the spies to Rahab. He had gone before His people and provided a way for them to enter the Promised Land; however, not only were the Israelites to have the benefit of this provision, but Rahab and her family would also be rescued. God's victories over the dreaded armies of their region were heard all through Jericho; God made sure of it. Rahab knew that God had protected the Israelites.

Are there ways that God has provided for you when you were not aware? Have you considered that God has gone before you? Rahab relinquished her fears to hide the spies; she trusted that God would take care of her and her family. She was a prostitute and lived inside the walls of Jericho; she had no status nor did she have the means to save herself and her family. But Rahab knew that God did. He was the sovereign God of the Israelites.

Rahab requested that if she hid them and allowed them time to spy out the land that she and her family be protected. God gave her the ability to have the courage to ask and receive protection. God gives His own what is necessary to be used by Him for His purposes. We can be assured that God reveals Himself and provides for His children. He is a mighty warrior who rescues His own.

Is there something that God is leading you to do that He alone is able to give you the courage to do? Have you asked Him?

✦

> "I BECAME A SERVANT OF THE GOSPEL BY THE GIFT OF GOD'S GRACE GIVEN ME BY THE WORKING OF HIS POWER." - EPHESIANS 3:7

**Read Joshua 2; Job 38**
In this second segment, what is the dilemma for Rahab? And for the Israelites?
Describe the issue at hand for Rahab and for the Israelites.

# RAHAB

DAY TWO - WHAT IS THE DILEMMA?

# RAHAB

DAY THREE - WHAT IS GOD'S RESCUE?

*God makes our steps bring His results*

God made it clear to Rahab that He is sovereign. He gave her the wisdom to know Him and the faith to believe that He would protect her and her family. Not only did God give Rahab the wherewithal, God gave her the steps to take to make it happen. What may we have to do that it will be necessary for God to give us the wisdom and the faith in order to accomplish it? Isn't it always the case? We always need the wisdom and the faith to carry out whatever it is that God wants us to do. There is nothing that we can do on our own. God gave Rahab the dependency on Him in order to carry out the plan.

The risks were great; Rahab and her family could die. However, Rahab was willing to make the sacrifice. God chose Rahab for purposes He knew beforehand. What does God know about us? He knows us from the inside out and loves us anyway.

God gave all that Rahab needed to accomplish this task. She relinquished her ideas of safety and security because she trusted the sovereign God of the universe. Only God gives us the heart to know Him, the eyes to see, and the ears to hear. God prepared Rahab for the sacrifice.

God created a way for His people to enter the land He had promised them. His ways are higher than our ways (Isaiah 55:8); His thoughts are not our own. He gives us the means to do works He created for us to do (Ephesians 2:10). Before creation, God gave gifts to us in order for us to produce good works in His name. Rahab, created to do good works, accomplished them for His name because God prepared her
every step of the way.

✦

> "I PRAY OUT OF HIS GLORIOUS RICHES HE MAY STRENGTHEN YOU WITH POWER THROUGH HIS SPIRIT IN YOUR INNER BEING..." - EPHESIANS 3:16

**Read Joshua 2; Proverbs 16**

In the third segment, what is God's rescue? How does God intervene for Rahab in the scripture passage, and how does God intervene for the Israelites? How does God show His care and provision?

# RAHAB

DAY THREE - WHAT IS GOD'S RESCUE?

# RAHAB

DAY FOUR - WHAT IS THE RESULT OF GOD'S RESCUE?

*God rewards the risk and the sacrifice made by His children*

God gave the spies the means to save Rahab and her family from harm, and they carried it out. God rewarded the sacrifice Rahab made when she hid the spies and risked her life. God knows the hearts of all; He wants each of His children to follow His heart, full of grace and truth. He sees the willingness of His child's heart to trust Him with the big and the little things of life, and it pleases Him. God saw the heart of a prostitute, His child Rahab. In God's eyes, she was His child, not a profession, a race, a woman of ill repute, but His own, created by Him for good works.

When we are willing to trust Him with our lives, God becomes our Father and Savior God. There is nothing He will not do to rescue us to save us, and when He does, there is nothing He will not do to continue to save us from ourselves, our sin, this fallen world. He pursues us with His lovingkindness, which is forever. God loves us, and we were always His plan.

Rahab knew this in her heart, and God responded with His lovingkindness to her and her family. She may have been hidden in the wall for most of her life at this point in history, but she would not remain so. Rahab took the risk to help the Israelites; she sacrificed her own needs for those of the spies. God had the spies honor her plea and grant her family deliverance from the battle with a place to live and grow old.

God keeps His promises, the big ones and the small ones. He is the God of promise and promise keeping. When He gave the Promised Land to His people, the Israelites, He gave them the way to follow and the courage to enter into it too. Rahab, integral to God's promise, is in the lineage of Jesus.

✦

> "(YOU) MAY HAVE POWER, TOGETHER WITH ALL THE LORD'S HOLY PEOPLE, TO GRASP HOW WIDE AND LONG AND HIGH AND DEEP IS THE LOVE OF CHRIST AND TO KNOW THAT THIS LOVE SURPASSES KNOWLEDGE THAT YOU MAY BE FILLED TO THE MEASURE OF ALL THE FULLNESS OF GOD." - EPHESIANS 3:18-19

**Read Joshua 6; James 1:12**

In this fourth segment, what is the result of God's rescue? What happens as a result of God's intervention in the lives of Rahab and also the lives of the Israelites?

# RAHAB

DAY FOUR - WHAT IS THE RESULT OF GOD'S RESCUE?

# RAHAB

DAY FIVE - WHAT IS THE "STORY FOR GOD'S GLORY?"

*God makes us His own to bring glory to His name*

Rahab brought glory to God's name. Just as she had heard of God Himself and His deliverance of His people, she helped Him deliver her and her family and the Israelites again in the battle of Jericho so that they could enter the Promised Land. God's name would be heard again and again throughout the land as His children entered the land God promised them with Joshua as their leader.

As the Israelites marched around Jericho and blew the trumpet just as God commanded, the walls came tumbling down. God gave them victory over Jericho. Rahab and her family were saved as were Joshua and the spies, the ones to whom God had made the promise many generations before. God's name is before all names; it is the name for His people, God's chosen ones. God chooses His children to bring glory to His name. What does this mean?

God's love and power are what the world needs. God made His love and power known to this fallen world through His Son, Jesus. He continues to reveal Himself to His creation, all His children, through those who commit their hearts to Him. The privilege He gives to each child who bears His name is to share His name and bring glory to Him with their lives.

God gave Rahab the opportunity to live out her acknowledgement of who He is, the God of the universe who is sovereign over all. She lived before God revealed Himself through His Only Son, Jesus, but she knew Him. Rahab was not chosen because of anything she was or did; God chose her because He loved her. He loves each of us. Are you willing to give Him your heart? Imagine what He may do with it.

✦

> **"FINALLY, BE STRONG IN THE LORD AND IN HIS MIGHTY POWER." - EPHESIANS 6:10**

**Read Joshua 6; Hebrews 11:6; Matthew 1:5**

What is the story for God's glory in Rahab's life? What happens in Rahab's life to make God the main character of her story? What happens in Rahab's story to demonstrate who God is and what He does for His children?

# RAHAB

DAY FIVE - WHAT IS THE "STORY FOR GOD'S GLORY?"

# RAHAB

DAY SIX - WHAT ARE GOD'S TRUTHS?

*Trusting God, a choice*

God's choosing Rahab was the beginning of the choice she had to make. When Rahab recognized that the spies were followers of God, sent by God to scout out the land for the Israelites, she made an agreement with them to hide them despite the danger she would be in for helping them. God chose Rahab to make this decision which would impact the future of His people. What has He chosen you to do?

I have a choice. It is to love Him with my whole heart, soul, mind, and strength. Yet, when I put myself, my plans, or my family and friends before the Lord, I am choosing another. God will help us to choose Him before all other things in our lives. May we ask Him to help us choose Him. May we seek Him while He may be found (Isaiah 55:6).

✦

> "BUT WHEN HE, THE SPIRIT OF TRUTH, COMES, HE WILL GUIDE YOU INTO ALL THE TRUTH."
> JOHN 16:13A

### Reflections
Reflect on the truths of God you have learned in Rahab's life. And your own?
How do we know God enabled Rahab to trust Him with herself and her family?
How was trusting God a choice for Rahab?

# RAHAB

DAY SIX - WHAT ARE GOD'S TRUTHS?

# A PERSPECTIVE
## CROSSING OVER INTO GOD'S NEW AND SPACIOUS PLACE

After making a significant step in trusting God, seemingly there are monumental obstacles blocking our way forward in faith. The new crossing into more of God in a life becomes the introduction to something that hinders the path. The barrier is real. The evil one does not want us to live more abundantly with God.

We see that this is also true of our twelve characters in this study. Abraham trusted God, and then he and Sarah could not conceive. Waiting became a huge part of the couple's journey with the Lord. David, anointed king of Israel by the prophet, Samuel, did not reign for fifteen years, and there were many dangers and snares which put him in harm's way by Saul. Joshua led his people into the Promised Land only to have to conquer the peoples already living there. We always have more "crossing over" to do; God allows hard things in order for us to know and depend on Him more, to know our need for Him, and to receive more of Him during our lives as His children.

We are able to be encouraged and reminded of the faithfulness of God in the lives of these characters in the Bible. They trusted God, and yet, they suffered and walked through difficult times. He assured them that they would not go without Him, nor would they ever not have His presence with them. This is our great hope and promise too; He will never leave us or forsake us.

The journeys God has marked out for us include hard times, and while we are in them, He comes along beside us in the trial, often carrying us and reminding us of who He is and what He does for us, His children. We remember from our own previous life experiences that this is true. He knows exactly what we are going through, and He is with us now and will continue to be, leading and guiding, strengthening and comforting, and providing just what we need when we need it. God goes before us on our journeys to show us the way, and more than that, to live with and within us while being our God He always has been and will be.

It was like this for us as a family moving to a new home, new school, with new friends and community. God had provided a miracle; He not only showed us the way but He also gave each of us the courage and faith to go with Him and enjoy what He had freely given us. Yet, we each had our moments of struggle and questions about the move. There is always trouble in the Promised Land, and God gives us what we need in battle. He fights it for us, and He wants us to trust Him more. The spacious place He provides is also the place we have to trust Him again and again. He never tires of teaching and reminding us of this truth. He is not going anywhere; we are. He loves us and comes to us as we are.

Trusting Him, which He also enables us to do, becomes the very vehicle by which He gives us the spacious place, more and more of Himself. Always moving us to a more spacious place, He loves us more than we imagine. His spacious place for us is bigger than our finite minds fathom.

Is it too much ado about us? Often, we confuse our study of God's word with a study of the knowledge of God. As we read scripture, we sometimes place more emphasis on the way we are to live than on a real yearning to know Him. We compare our lives to the lives of characters in the Bible, and we miss the real teaching. God in His word teaches us about each of His Biblical characters, because He knows that we need to know Him more. As we take a look at these individual's lives, God draws us to Himself to know more about Him, who He is, and what He does in the lives of His children.

The thrust of our work here on earth is to know Him more. Why not do it when we study His word too, even if it happens also to show us themes of our own lives. What if we were to focus on God in these stories and in our own? "Who is He" in these real-life Biblical characters' stories? "Who is He" in our own lives?

These real-life characters give us much to learn; they demonstrate faithfulness to the Lord and many more times, sinfulness and rebelliousness in their ways. I believe we, in summary, gain a lot from knowing that they are sinful and faithful and all in between. It is of great value to see the real lives of our Biblical ancestors in the faith; however, we must not miss the greater benefit of knowing our Lord more.

✦

In what ways do you make your life more about you?

PART IV

# ELIZABETH

GOD'S HEART

MORE OF GOD IN OUR LIVES AND STORIES

IN THE TIME OF HEROD KING OF JUDEA THERE WAS A PRIEST NAMED ZECHARIAH, WHO BELONGED TO THE PRIESTLY DIVISION OF ABIJAH; HIS WIFE ELIZABETH WAS ALSO A DESCENDANT OF AARON. BOTH OF THEM WERE RIGHTEOUS IN THE SIGHT OF GOD, OBSERVING ALL THE LORD'S COMMANDS AND DECREES BLAMELESSLY. BUT THEY WERE CHILDLESS BECAUSE ELIZABETH WAS NOT ABLE TO CONCEIVE, AND THEY WERE BOTH VERY OLD.

AT THAT TIME MARY GOT READY AND HURRIED TO A TOWN IN THE HILL COUNTRY OF JUDEA, WHERE SHE ENTERED ZECHARIAH'S HOME AND GREETED ELIZABETH. WHEN ELIZABETH HEARD MARY'S GREETING, THE BABY LEAPED IN HER WOMB, AND ELIZABETH WAS FILLED WITH THE HOLY SPIRIT. IN A LOUD VOICE SHE EXCLAIMED: "BLESSED ARE YOU AMONG WOMEN, AND BLESSED IS THE CHILD YOU WILL BEAR! BUT WHY AM I SO FAVORED, THAT THE MOTHER OF MY LORD SHOULD COME TO ME? AS SOON AS THE SOUND OF YOUR GREETING REACHED MY EARS, THE BABY IN MY WOMB LEAPED FOR JOY. BLESSED IS SHE WHO HAS BELIEVED THAT THE LORD WOULD FULFILL HIS PROMISES TO HER!

LUKE 1:5-7; 39-45

## PART IV
# ELIZABETH
GOD'S HEART

God does more than we ask or imagine. Elizabeth and Zechariah were childless, and Elizabeth persisted in prayer for a son. God heard her. He called the couple "blameless and righteous." Can you imagine? And then for their prayers not to be answered. It was a constant humiliation to the couple; yet, they persevered because God gave them the capacity to do so.

God answered their prayers for a son in John the Baptist. Imagine that! The precursor to Jesus! Elizabeth and Zechariah were astounded at God's provision.

Are we astounded at God's provision?

✦

**Mystery**
Being called "blameless and righteous" is a mystery, and yet, one that God calls us to in Jesus' name when we become His children and follow Him.

**Power**
God gave the two of them faithfulness in prayer and in their lives with Him.

**Paradox**
Elizabeth and Zechariah were holy in God's sight. They had not conceived, but God has a plan that is beyond our comprehension. It is for good!

The Power of the Resurrection in Elizabeth's Life

# ELIZABETH

DAY ONE - WHO IS GOD?

*God's heart for us is for us to be righteous and blameless, and He has provided the way in Jesus*

The scripture describes Zechariah and Elizabeth as righteous and blameless before the Lord. In other words, God called Zechariah, the priest, and his wife, Elizabeth, "right with God." As God's children, we are too. What an awesome privilege! The only path to righteousness is through the eyes of the Lord; He calls each child of His "righteous" when we follow Him. God knew the hearts of his servants, Zechariah and Elizabeth.

God also knew their pain and disgrace in their community from childlessness. An angel announces to Zechariah that he and Elizabeth would have a son. God comes to Zechariah in the temple through an angel of the Lord. They had been praying for a long time for this news.
The truth is that God comes. God answers our prayers.

What is happening in your life about which you have cried out to God? If you haven't, will you? God's heart is for us. He knows our longings and our circumstances; He knows every desire of the heart. As we call on Him, may we know that He hears us. His lovingkindness meets us just as He met Elizabeth and Zechariah as they cried out to Him about their dilemma.

✦

> "I PRAY THAT THE EYES OF YOUR HEART MAY BE ENLIGHTENED IN ORDER THAT YOU MAY KNOW THE HOPE TO WHICH HE HAS CALLED YOU, THE RICHES OF HIS GLORIOUS INHERITANCE IN HIS HOLY PEOPLE, AND HIS INCOMPARABLY GREAT POWER FOR US WHO BELIEVE. THAT POWER IS THE SAME AS THE MIGHTY STRENGTH HE EXERTED WHEN HE RAISED CHRIST FROM THE DEAD AND SEATED HIM AT HIS RIGHT HAND IN THE HEAVENLY REALMS ..." - EPHESIANS 1:18-20

**Read Luke 1**
Who is God in this scripture passage? How does He show up in Elizabeth and Zechariah's life?

# ELIZABETH

DAY ONE - WHO IS GOD?

The Power of The Resurrection in Elizabeth's Life

# ELIZABETH

DAY TWO - WHAT IS THE DILEMMA?

*God knows the hearts of His children. He shows up to come along beside them to provide*

God knew the turmoil and disgrace of Zechariah and Elizabeth, especially as they served as a priest and priest's wife. He knew what a son would bring to them and to their community. God gives out of His lovingkindness; He knows our hearts and shows up to walk beside and through our difficulties and pain. God knew Elizabeth's disgrace as a barren woman.

God also knew that Zechariah would respond as he did to the angel. God answers in greater measure than we ask. Zechariah, much like we are at times, doubted the angel's news. Not trusting the Lord's provision created a new situation for Zechariah: he became mute. It was not until the baby was born that he regained his voice.

How are you not trusting in the Lord to come along beside you? Is there an answer that you have not received? Perhaps, God has given it and you have not trusted Him in it. Just as Zechariah, you may not believe that God will give you the very thing for which you have asked of Him. God pursues us in order to come with us and guide us through; sometimes we wrestle with Him instead of resting in Him. What have you not laid to rest at His feet?

✦

> "I BECAME A SERVANT OF THE GOSPEL BY THE GIFT OF GOD'S GRACE GIVEN ME BY THE WORKING OF HIS POWER. - EPHESIANS 3:7

**Read Luke 1; Psalm 42**

In this second day of scripture reading, what is the dilemma for Elizabeth and Zechariah?

# ELIZABETH

DAY TWO - WHAT IS THE DILEMMA?

# ELIZABETH

DAY THREE - WHAT IS GOD'S RESCUE?

*God answers our prayers in greater ways than we imagine*

God hears and answers our prayers and provides more than we ask or imagine (Ephesians 3:19-20). The angel tells Zechariah that their son would be "in the spirit and power of Elijah." Their son would "turn the hearts of parents to their children" and "the disobedient to the wisdom of the righteous" and "would make ready a people prepared for the Lord." (Luke 1:15-16) Imagine if you were told that your son would be like Elijah. Even in Zechariah's role as a priest, it had to be a jolt to hear this news. Yet, the Lord sent his angel to reveal the wonderful news to the priest, his servant. The lovingkindness of the Lord provides in wonderful ways. Surely, we have no need to doubt Him.

Elizabeth becomes pregnant and knew it was from the Lord. She says, "The Lord has done this for me." God took away her disgrace among the people with the news of a child. (Luke 1:15-16) God gave Elizabeth a heart to receive this wonderful news. His gift of a Son, who was on the way, and her receiving the news in the way that she did was also a gift. How may we be ready to receive His answers? Do we know that as His children, He has taken away the disgrace and shame of our former selves and lives as sinners in need of a Savior?

Elizabeth knew the Savior, our Father God, in Jesus Christ. In her long years of praying for a child, God revealed Himself to her. She knew her Father God and His lovingkindness because He had shown her His heart. May we know His heart for us and expect His lovingkindness in ways we have never received before.

✦

> "I PRAY OUT OF HIS GLORIOUS RICHES HE MAY STRENGTHEN YOU WITH POWER THROUGH HIS SPIRIT IN YOUR INNER BEING..." - EPHESIANS 3:16

**Read Luke 1; Psalm 40**
In this third segment, what is God's rescue for Elizabeth? How does He provide for Elizabeth?

# ELIZABETH

DAY THREE - WHAT IS GOD'S RESCUE?

# ELIZABETH

## DAY FOUR - WHAT IS THE RESULT OF GOD'S RESCUE?

*God speaks through the stories of His people*

What a story Elizabeth has! She gives birth to the messenger before Jesus, John the Baptist, who spread the news of Jesus' coming. Elizabeth and Zechariah's son would be a joy and delight to them and to the world; he would be filled with the Holy Spirit and bring many people to the Lord.

As Elizabeth gave birth, all rejoiced in the Lord. Their hopes were tied to Elizabeth and Zechariah's hopes. God gives each of His children a story to be shared and told. God speaks through His angel, Gabriel. Zachariah eventually speaks when the Lord gives him his voice back. Elizabeth speaks of her Lord and how He has answered her prayer. The community speaks their joy and gratitude for the Lord in bringing a son to their priest and priest's wife. God gives us validations of His answers to prayer too. They become grace and truth to all of the persons around us. God speaks through our stories of Him.

It is His Name to be proclaimed. It is in His name that we are called children of God. And it is for His name that we gather and share and pass on the stories of our great God.

What is your story? How has God brought you through? Are you passing it on?

✦

> "(YOU) MAY HAVE POWER, TOGETHER WITH ALL THE LORD'S HOLY PEOPLE, TO GRASP HOW WIDE AND LONG AND HIGH AND DEEP IS THE LOVE OF CHRIST AND TO KNOW THAT THIS LOVE SURPASSES KNOWLEDGE THAT YOU MAY BE FILLED TO THE MEASURE OF ALL THE FULLNESS OF GOD" - EPHESIANS 3:18-19

**Read Luke 1; Psalm 71**
In this fourth segment, what is the result of the Lord's rescue for Elizabeth and Zechariah?

# ELIZABETH

DAY FOUR - WHAT IS THE RESULT OF GOD'S RESCUE?

# ELIZABETH

DAY FIVE - WHAT IS THE "STORY FOR GOD'S GLORY?"

*God gives us His name; He then gives us a story to be shared in and for His name*

Elizabeth and Zechariah were God's children, priests of the Lord. In their long years of childlessness, God, in His great mercy and truth, gave them a story for the ages, ours to behold and cherish for the generations. And the Lord sent an angel to bring the good news to them. God always shows up. He always provides His lovingkindness; it is who He is and what He does for His beloved.

Despite our doubting and not trusting Him for answers to us, God comes. In and for His great name, He shares His name with us. And He gives us the privilege to go out and share the story He has begun in us. For God's name is above all others. He is God; there is no other.

What do you know the Lord is doing in your life? Have you received from Him a hard thing? Are you embracing it? What might there be in store for you through this difficulty? More of Him?

Who are you? What is your story? What truth is God giving you with your unfolding story?

✦

> "FINALLY, BE STRONG IN THE LORD AND IN HIS MIGHTY POWER."
> - EPHESIANS 6:10

### Read Luke 1

How do Mary's Song and Zechariah's Prophecy reveal God's story for His glory in Elizabeth's life? What do these two passages proclaim about who God is? How is God the main character in Elizabeth and Zechariah's story, the story for God's glory?

# ELIZABETH

DAY FIVE - WHAT IS THE "STORY FOR GOD'S GLORY?"

The Power of The Resurrection in Elizabeth's Life

# ELIZABETH

DAY SIX - WHAT ARE GOD'S TRUTHS?

*Trusting God with our dreams*

How did Elizabeth manage it— a great dream surrendered to God? I believe that God gave Elizabeth the wherewithal to trust Him. She prayed diligently day after day for a child. In addition to His hearing her need for faith, He also gave to Elizabeth her heart's desire. I want to lay down my dreams to God too. What are yours? What is your greatest hope and dream on this earth?

God gave Elizabeth the means to lay down her greatest dream of having a baby and trust Him with it. May I lay down my dreams for the ability to serve God through relationships and writing and teaching so that His perfect plan for such a time as this may be fulfilled to His glory.

✦

> "BUT WHEN HE, THE SPIRIT OF TRUTH, COMES, HE WILL GUIDE YOU INTO ALL THE TRUTH" - JOHN 16:13A

### Reflection

In this sixth segment, what truths have you learned from Elizabeth's story? What did God enable Elizabeth to do? Have you asked God to give you the means to trust Him with your own dreams?

# ELIZABETH

DAY SIX - WHAT ARE GOD'S TRUTHS?

✦

The Power of The Resurrection in Elizabeth's Life

# A PERSPECTIVE
BY FAITH

We learn a lot about God's people in His word. The author of Hebrews goes into great detail about many of the great children of God in the Bible in chapter 11. For each of the named persons, the author says that they did the things they did, fought the battles they fought, moved here and there, left their homes, and kept persevering in their journeys on earth "by faith." By faith in whom? It was by their faith in the God of the universe, Jesus Christ, that they traveled, persevered, and crossed over many obstacles. We have the same mission for such a time as this. Are we not like our ancestors in the faith that we must also choose to walk by faith? Who is He who gives us the journey and the faith in which to go the way He marked out for us? We must go the journey by faith just as our ancestors did. God taught them the way to go as they trusted Him for the journey. As we look at their lives and stories, by faith we ask our Lord Jesus Christ to teach us through them. What does He want us to know about who He is and how much He loves us?

Furthermore, in chapter 12 the author of Hebrews describes and gives us instruction as to how we may travel by faith on this journey with God on earth. He reminds us of the ones who have gone before us, "the great cloud of witnesses." And he emboldens us with the extraordinary words which speak to us about the truth of living as children of God in a fallen world. We are to throw off all that may hinder us, our sin and all else that entangles us along the way. The author clearly states to persevere in this race by keeping our focus upon the One who has already paved the way for us, Jesus Christ, who died because He loved us so much. While giving us instructions about how to walk by faith, the author makes his own understanding known of the pitfalls and the dangers as we, God's children, continue on by faith. Our Lord's compassion, lovingkindness, and power enable each of us as we step out in faith, and He gives us the capacity not to grow weary or lose heart and helps us to keep our focus on Him, who is our story.

Who is God in Peter's life, Abraham's, Rahab's, Elizabeth's, or Deborah's? What does God want us to know about Himself and His character? Each of these people of the Bible had flaws and a sin nature, and in many ways, they were hindered and entangled along the way of their lives. But who is God in their life and story? How does it help you to study God's word in this person's story in order to know God better in your life and story? Not to be distracted by the person's character or lack thereof, we will see who God is and what He does with and for His children. Are we like them? Most of the lot from what we see in their descriptions were unlikely candidates, flawed, wandering, and helpless, and in other words, each has a great need for the Lord. We too are sinful, lacking, and so desperately needing the Lord even when we do not know it; yet, God chooses us, you and me, to be His children and to do His work. He is intentional. It is not a whim. He wants you; He wants me. He wants us to be in relationship with Him.

By faith we know Him more and more through His word. His presence, His promises, His purpose, and His provision come into focus through studying, particularly as we study the lives of His children in His word. We know what God cares about: His love for us is higher, deeper, wider, longer than we know, and He does more than we ask or imagine (Ephesians 3:14-21).

*By faith, the pilgrimage...*
God leads us on a pilgrimage. He is our destination and our home while we travel. It is in our lack that we find Him over and over again. He covers us when at rest and when we step out; He is in the tears and desert, but also in the joy which comes and in the river of life. We do not go without Him, nor do we rest on our own. I am overwhelmed by His presence and the design to draw us near to Him. Our Creator brings us close to live in union with Him at all times; we cannot go anywhere without Him, nor would we want to if we only knew the length, depth, height, and width of His love. Yet, He comes to us and pursues us so that we may know. There is nothing lost to Him. God creates new out of nothing and restores our mess with His imagination with His grace and truth. Our pilgrimage is nothing less than remarkable in His love and power.

Because the Lord supplies what we need on this pilgrimage, we have the strength to walk with Him through the hard things. It says in Psalm 84 that we go from "strength to strength." By faith we step out to find His strength for each moment of each day. It is in the faith to step out on the pilgrimage we know His power. He carries us through the desert, the tears, and the many obstacles along the way. When we are striving in our own strength on the pilgrimage of life, we have little resources to continue; yet, with God by faith we have all we need. On the long haul, a pilgrimage, God has the trail marked out; we may let go and let Him lead, as we rely upon His strength and resources for the journey.

God is preparing us for the long haul, not the short term, and He is present with us for every bit. We want all to be set aright at the moment when He has the longer perspective in mind. He created us for His purposes and His name for the world to know Him. How do we know in a second the long perspective? We can't, and we don't, but we often strive for it. By faith we may ask for God's perspective. And by faith we will know Him on the pilgrimage as He answers. God created us for the pilgrimage. We may not have considered our lives a pilgrimage; yet, God in His compassion and creativity gives us just what we need for the journey. And while on the journey, He prepares us for each new thing He has in mind and also helps us leave behind what we do not need as we go. As we set our focus on Him, all other fades away, because He sharpens our focus and provides for all else. We are His, and as this truth comes into view for us, the pilgrimage is right and true. All becomes part of His plan for us to know Him and to become one with Him.

As we follow our ancestors' pilgrimages, let us look for the God of the universe and His presence, promises, provision, and purpose in their lives. Who is the God of our fathers?

How did He let Himself be known to them? What did He promise them and how did He provide for them? Has he set you on a pilgrimage? If you do not know your pilgrimage, will you ask God? Have you known God's presence and if not, will you ask Him? How have you been provided for in your life or pilgrimage? Do you know the God of promise? We see the promises God makes to His children through these stories of our ancestors. For what purpose did God create our ancestors and how did they live out His God-given purpose on their pilgrimages? Do you know the purpose for which God made you? God made you for a purpose, one that is greater than you imagine.

Pilgrimage by faith:
- We know the One who knows the way even when we don't
- We keep moving in the direction of the One who knows the way
- It may be the long haul; only He knows
- We get up each day and know that there is purpose in the day
- We know for whom we are going, living, making each step
- With each trial or triumph, He provides what we need; He provides the daily needs too
- The destination is totally worth it; He is the destination, and we have Him along the way

Focusing on Jesus is what guides the pilgrimage:
- Keeping in step with Jesus
    - Living – daily work and interruptions
    - Daily disciplines – prayer, bible study, service
    - Fellowship with Him and with others
- Through suffering and joy of daily living
    - Turning toward Jesus for letting them go and rejoicing in all
    - Gratitude for the day and what it brings and praising Him for all
    - Standing in Him with the armor of God
- Learning and remembering the Lord has taken care of you and yours


Have you made the step of faith to follow Jesus?

_____
_____
_____
_____
_____
_____

What is a step of faith that you have taken recently? How might you ask God to show and guide you through a new step of faith?

PART V

# DEBORAH

GOD'S MIND

MORE OF GOD IN OUR LIVES AND STORIES

AGAIN THE ISRAELITES DID EVIL IN THE EYES OF THE LORD, NOW THAT EHUD WAS DEAD. SO THE LORD SOLD THEM INTO THE HANDS OF JABIN KING OF CANAAN, WHO REIGNED IN HAZOR. SISERA, THE COMMANDER OF HIS ARMY, WAS BASED IN HAROSHETH HAGGOYIM. BECAUSE HE HAD NINE HUNDRED CHARIOTS FITTED WITH IRON AND HAD CRUELLY OPPRESSED THE ISRAELITES FOR TWENTY YEARS, THEY CRIED TO THE LORD FOR HELP. NOW DEBORAH, A PROPHET, THE WIFE OF LAPPIDOTH, WAS LEADING ISRAEL AT THAT TIME. SHE HELD COURT UNDER THE PALM OF DEBORAH BETWEEN RAMAH AND BETHEL IN THE HILL COUNTRY OF EPHRAIM, AND THE ISRAELITES WENT UP TO HER TO HAVE THEIR DISPUTES DECIDED.

JUDGES 4:1-5

## PART V
# DEBORAH
GOD'S MIND

God uses what is not of this world to dismay those in the world. He confounds and perplexes. It is He who reigns and chooses. God chose Deborah, a woman, to judge, to prophesy, and to lead Israel's army into battle. She was a woman in a man's world, so to speak, and God gave her the mind of Christ.

Deborah chose to listen and know God's wisdom to call upon Him for her decisions for her people. God showed her the way in that day; He had given her a heart for Him. He empowered her in His ways in order to protect His people.

✦

**Mystery**
God uses what is not of this world to confound the world. Deborah definitely drew upon the power, not of this world, but of her Father God.

**Power**
It was only the power of the resurrection that saved Israel against the armies of Sisera and Sisera himself. Deborah got the win but knew to whom the win belonged.

**Paradox**
It is the things of the world which mislead; God's ways lead to His victory. A woman in a man's world, Deborah, knew the wisdom of God and lived by it, because God had enabled her to do so.

The Power of the Resurrection in Deborah's Life

# DEBORAH

## DAY ONE - WHO IS GOD?

*God creates each child, and for each one who chooses to follow Him, He gives a mind for Him*

God is the giver of all good things; He bestows on each of His creation His unique image. Deborah knew the Lord. She was a prophet, judge, and leader anointed by God to govern and rule. She was in a position of power, and she followed the Lord's wisdom as she led her people.

Deborah knew that God was the giver of all we are and have; she lived a life in awe of the One who placed her right where she was. During this time, Israel was being oppressed by the King of Canaan, Jabin. Deborah sent for Barak and told him that God would lead the armies of Sisera into their hands, that they would defeat their enemy. Barak, the Israelites' first in command of the army, would not lead them without her going with them. Deborah assured him she would go with him, but that the honor would belong to a woman. The Lord would deliver them from their enemies.

Deborah received from the Lord a mind to follow Him with wisdom and courage. She knew the dire consequences without her Lord's intervention. Her direction came from Him, the One who endowed her with the position and capacity to deliver her people from the enemy. Barak chose to keep her close and to have her lead them into battle. The scripture does not explain his reasons, except that he knew that she had the mind of God with her. Perhaps, this is the lesson in the text; we must know Him in order to do the things He asks of us. God gives us the capacity to follow His word when we step out with Him. Deborah knew the wisdom of the Lord because she had depended on Him for it.

God gives us the capacity to know Him and to have the mind of Christ. Have you taken the first step to know Him by asking Jesus into your life? For what do you need God's wisdom? Are you seeking Him?

---

> "I PRAY THAT THE EYES OF YOUR HEART MAY BE ENLIGHTENED IN ORDER THAT YOU MAY KNOW THE HOPE TO WHICH HE HAS CALLED YOU, THE RICHES OF HIS GLORIOUS INHERITANCE IN HIS HOLY PEOPLE, AND HIS INCOMPARABLY GREAT POWER FOR US WHO BELIEVE. THAT POWER IS THE SAME AS THE MIGHTY STRENGTH HE EXERTED WHEN HE RAISED CHRIST FROM THE DEAD AND SEATED HIM AT HIS RIGHT HAND IN THE HEAVENLY REALMS ..." - EPHESIANS 1:18-20

**Read Judges 4; Proverbs 3**
In this first segment, who is God? Who is He?

# DEBORAH

DAY ONE - WHO IS GOD?

# DEBORAH

DAY TWO - WHAT IS THE DILEMMA?

*God gives us the mind of Christ and the means to receive it*

Deborah received God's anointing with wisdom. With the mind of Christ, she followed through with His guidance and assurance during battle. With each step, she listened to God, received His instruction, and in turn did as He said. Deborah knew that it was He who delivered the Israelites.

God demonstrates His grace in provision for His people again. Throughout history God shows up not only to rescue His children but also to provide what they need in the moment. The Israelites needed a strong and courageous leader to guide them into battle to defeat the enemy. The chosen one, a woman, was anointed by God, which again was His grace for His people. We don't know why Barak chose as he did, but we know that the Lord provided.

God gave Deborah the confidence and assurance in addition to wisdom, strength, and courage to proceed in battle. Her instructions to Barak and his follow through with her guidance, the Lord's, led them into victory.

God gives confidence in Him and the assurance to receive it. Do you have what you need to follow Him?

✦

> "I BECAME A SERVANT OF THE GOSPEL BY THE GIFT OF GOD'S GRACE GIVEN ME BY THE WORKING OF HIS POWER." - EPHESIANS 3:7

**Read Judges 4; Proverbs 1**
In this second segment, what is the dilemma?

# DEBORAH

DAY TWO - WHAT IS THE DILEMMA?

# DEBORAH

DAY THREE - WHAT IS GOD'S RESCUE?

*God is in the details*

How is it that we feel that God does not consider the details of our lives? In this story of Deborah's life and the lives of the Israelites, God gives the instructions to defeat the enemy. God not only shows up in Deborah's life but also through Deborah to Barak, the Israelites, and to their enemies and their enemies' leaders. God is in the details of our lives.

God showed up to save His people through the detailed instructions of Deborah in her command of the army. God's wise counsel came in the person of Deborah as judge and prophet to the people of Israel. God comes in the person of Jesus Christ for each of us to know Him and to receive all of Him for our lives. Are there battles we are attempting to fight without the Lord? Even through God already knows the intricacies of our lives and hearts, He tells us to share them with Him by crying out to Him in prayer.

Our thoughts are not His thoughts, nor are our ways His ways (Isaiah 55:8). Yet, God in Christ Jesus gives us His mind through the Holy Spirit. Are we sharing our hearts and minds with Him? There isn't anything too small or large for Him. There is nothing too hard. God is the God of the impossible. May we ask Him.

✦

> "I PRAY OUT OF HIS GLORIOUS RICHES HE MAY STRENGTHEN YOU WITH POWER THROUGH HIS SPIRIT IN YOUR INNER BEING..." - EPHESIANS 3:16

**Read Judges 4; Isaiah 55:8-9; Proverbs 2**

In this third segment, what is God's rescue? Describe the characters and their responses to God.

# DEBORAH

DAY THREE - WHAT IS GOD'S RESCUE?

# DEBORAH

## DAY FOUR - WHAT IS THE RESULT OF GOD'S RESCUE?

*God allows the hardships in each of our lives to grow us up in our faith and for the world to see and know Him*

God's wisdom is available to each of His children to receive and to follow. He allows our difficult circumstances so that we may depend on Him for everything we need. During the trying time of fighting the enemies of Israel, Deborah had to depend on the Lord for each approach, each involvement, and every step of every battle. She sought the Lord with her dilemma with the enemy and her interaction with Barak.

The Lord is Deborah's story. He delivered them from the enemy, Jabin and Sisera, through her leadership. How often does the world place honor on an individual? It is part and parcel of our culture to look at human beings as our heroes. God is the author and sustainer of our faith. He goes before us into battle. He leads us through it. And He provides the means to victory. Sometimes it is in the form of a leader like Deborah whose story in His word describes so clearly the hand of God and His provision in their times of trouble. As she told Barak, she would get the human honor of their victory; yet, she knew whom the ultimate provider of the victory would be.

God gives us the mind of Christ in order to fulfill the purposes for which He made us. It is God's hand who places us, His children, in positions of authority and any other positions to honor Him. Do we give credit to Him when we receive the accolades of our positions?

✦

> "(YOU) MAY HAVE POWER, TOGETHER WITH ALL THE LORD'S HOLY PEOPLE, TO GRASP HOW WIDE AND LONG AND HIGH AND DEEP IS THE LOVE OF CHRIST AND TO KNOW THAT THIS LOVE SURPASSES KNOWLEDGE THAT YOU MAY BE FILLED TO THE MEASURE OF ALL THE FULLNESS OF GOD" - EPHESIANS 3:18-19

**Read Judges 4; Daniel 2:20-23**
In this fourth segment, what is the result of God's rescue? Who receives God's rescue?

# DEBORAH

DAY FOUR - WHAT IS THE RESULT OF GOD'S RESCUE?

The Power of The Resurrection in Deborah's Life

# DEBORAH

DAY FIVE - WHAT IS THE "STORY FOR GOD'S GLORY?"

*God gives us the privilege as His children to bring honor to His name*

This victory during the time of Deborah's leadership brought peace to the land for forty years. God again provided for His people through the life of His servant, Deborah. Each of us has a purpose given by God before the creation of the world.

Deborah's life honored God. God used her anointing to show the world who He is, the One who rescues and provides for us because He loves us so much. He bestows upon each of His own the ability to serve Him with a purpose uniquely given. Through Deborah, who served God with her life and leadership capacity, God showed the world how He would deliver the Israelites from their enemies.

The scripture includes the song of Deborah and Barak in Judges 5. It demonstrates the power of the love of God for His children. As His own, we are given the privilege of being part of His story for all the world to see. Deborah gives us a glimpse of the anointing of God in a life. Despite the rules or views of the world around you, just as Deborah lived and led in a man's world, God can use you to bring about His purposes if you allow Him to lead and guide your life. What privilege awaits you to honor God with your life?

✦

> "FINALLY, BE STRONG IN THE LORD AND IN HIS MIGHTY POWER."
> - EPHESIANS 6:10

**Read Judges 5 (Deborah's song)**

What is the story for God's glory in Deborah's life? How does she describe what the Lord has done in her life and the lives of the Israelites? How would you describe what God has done in your own life?

# DEBORAH

DAY FIVE - WHAT IS THE "STORY FOR GOD'S GLORY?"

# DEBORAH

DAY SIX - WHAT ARE GOD'S TRUTHS?

*Trusting God in the battle*

God gives us the means to think and to follow Him as He did Deborah. His ways and thoughts are higher than ours. He gave Deborah the mind to discern His instruction and His ways in governing the people and in leading them into battle.

I need Him to help me to train my thoughts, to focus on Him, to seek Him in everything, and to trust Him, because He is faithful in all He is and does. I can rely on Him for wisdom and to help me have the mind of Christ. Am I surrendering my thoughts to Him? Have I fixed my mind on Jesus?

What might I ask the Lord for my mind? Instruction? Thoughts and ways? Wisdom? Obedience in mind and spirit?

✦

> "BUT WHEN HE, THE SPIRIT OF TRUTH, COMES, HE WILL GUIDE YOU INTO ALL THE TRUTH"
> - JOHN 16:13A

### Reflections

In this sixth segment, what truths did you learn about God from Deborah's story? Describe "trusting God in the battle" from this account of Deborah's life. Are you trusting God in the battle?

# DEBORAH

DAY SIX - WHAT ARE GOD'S TRUTHS?

# A PERSPECTIVE
WHO IS GOD AND HOW DO WE MEET HIM?

God awakens us to know Him, our heavenly Father, the Lord, Jesus Christ. It is a gift of God's grace that Jesus became the One who died and rose and lives to give us eternal life with Him. Through the Holy Spirit, God strengthens us in our inner being and gives us faith to follow Him, to acknowledge Him as the One true God, our Savior, to confess that we are sinners and need Him in our lives, and to let go of ourselves and our sin to Him to save us. In this same way, we have the capacity of the Holy Spirit to live in fellowship with others and receive more and more of Him, the abundant life in Jesus Christ. It is in the power of the Holy Spirit that we are able as followers of Jesus to live out our lives in this fallen world, to endure pain and suffering, and to persevere through persecution. Our forefathers of the faith taught us, as do our fellow journeymen in the faith, that with the Holy Spirit living within us that we have joy and peace as we make our way, even in the midst of trial and struggle. It is in these times that we depend on Him more and know Him in ways we would not have known without the difficulties and hardships. God shows up in our lives. He meets us in the place where we are. As we find and know God, our Lord Jesus Christ, we also come to know who we are and who we are to Him.

As we consider the life of a follower of Jesus, we have many examples in God's word to instruct us. In the life stories of our forefathers of the faith, we may ponder:

- Who does God say He is? What does God say He will do?
- How is one awakened to God? To sin and the need for grace?
- What part does suffering play in coming to know God?
- What was God willing to suffer to demonstrate His love for us?

And for us personally:
- Where are you now in your life (of faith or without faith)?
- Is your God large or small? How do you know which one He may be to you?
- How does your view of God change as you get into (read, study, stay) His word?
- As you read, study, or stay in His word, what does the scripture demonstrate about the character of God and His attributes?
- What is the first place you go when you are in pain or suffering? What does God's word say about suffering? Can we get through life without it?
- In the life of God's children, how big a part does suffering play? What part does God play in it?
- What part does prayer play in your relationship with God?
- What makes us avoid pain? How does an accurate Biblical view of God help us with avoidance, running from, controlling, fixing the difficulty?

As we go through life, we learn that we get to know God in our pain, our hard times, our struggles. Yet, we still find suffering an unfamiliar, untraveled, and unwelcomed path. God shows up and shows us His compassion, comfort, grace, mercy, kindness, love, guidance, wisdom, and healing, just to name a few. He is the author of our faith and the sustainer of our souls; He has our best interests at heart.

"Who is He?" is the question for every circumstance, whether we are suffering or not. When we start with this question, when we seek Him in all things, we find Him. He is faithful always. There is nothing too hard for Him, especially when our circumstances or consequences loom large. How have you handled hard times in the past? Do you go to God first, second, or last?

Until we have suffering, we do not know how we will handle it. It is in the hard times that we come to know we need God. We come to the end of ourselves, the end of our ways and means of handling life. With suffering we must live in it. When we cry out to God, He comes. He is already pursuing us with His love and waiting for us to come. As we draw near to Him, He draws near to us.

It is only through living life, the mundane, the daily, the ups and downs, that we know Him. Often, we live as though we must attain our way, but with God, we do not. He has already attained all that we need or want in Jesus Christ. In order to live the life that God has imagined for each of us, we must receive it. He has already written it. Leaning into Him, letting go of all else, we know Him through all parts of our lives, especially the suffering. As we trust God with our lives and receive the life God has written for us, He makes Himself known to us. It is beyond our imagination and for His glory.

*A little note: God allows hardship, pain, and suffering in our lives in this fallen world. As we trust Him as the Lord and Savior of our lives, He brings good in our lives through the suffering. He carries us through, He shows us the way, and He changes our view of who He is and what He does.*

How might you ask the Lord for a new view? A fresh look? How might you look at your struggles differently?

When difficulty comes in the future, how will you view it by the power of the resurrection?

PART VI

# PAUL

GOD'S GRACE

MORE OF GOD IN OUR LIVES AND STORIES

PRAISE BE TO THE GOD AND FATHER OF OUR LORD JESUS CHRIST, WHO HAS BLESSED US IN THE HEAVENLY REALMS WITH EVERY SPIRITUAL BLESSING IN CHRIST. FOR HE CHOSE US IN HIM BEFORE THE CREATION OF THE WORLD TO BE HOLY AND BLAMELESS IN HIS SIGHT. IN LOVE HE PREDESTINED US FOR ADOPTION TO SONSHIP THROUGH JESUS CHRIST, IN ACCORDANCE WITH HIS PLEASURE AND WILL— TO THE PRAISE OF HIS GLORIOUS GRACE, WHICH HE HAS FREELY GIVEN US IN THE ONE HE LOVES. IN HIM WE HAVE REDEMPTION THROUGH HIS BLOOD, THE FORGIVENESS OF SINS, IN ACCORDANCE WITH THE RICHES OF GOD'S GRACE THAT HE LAVISHED ON US. WITH ALL WISDOM AND UNDERSTANDING, HE MADE KNOWN TO US THE MYSTERY OF HIS WILL ACCORDING TO HIS GOOD PLEASURE, WHICH HE PURPOSED IN CHRIST, TO BE PUT INTO EFFECT WHEN THE TIMES REACH THEIR FULFILLMENT—TO BRING UNITY TO ALL THINGS IN HEAVEN AND ON EARTH UNDER CHRIST. IN HIM WE WERE ALSO CHOSEN, HAVING BEEN PREDESTINED ACCORDING TO THE PLAN OF HIM WHO WORKS OUT EVERYTHING IN CONFORMITY WITH THE PURPOSE OF HIS WILL, IN ORDER THAT WE, WHO WERE THE FIRST TO PUT OUR HOPE IN CHRIST, MIGHT BE FOR THE PRAISE OF HIS GLORY. AND YOU ALSO WERE INCLUDED IN CHRIST WHEN YOU HEARD THE MESSAGE OF TRUTH, THE GOSPEL OF YOUR SALVATION. WHEN YOU BELIEVED, YOU WERE MARKED IN HIM WITH A SEAL, THE PROMISED HOLY SPIRIT, WHO IS A DEPOSIT GUARANTEEING OUR INHERITANCE UNTIL THE REDEMPTION OF THOSE WHO ARE GOD'S POSSESSION —TO THE PRAISE OF HIS GLORY.

EPHESIANS 1:3-14

PART VI

# PAUL

GOD'S GRACE

God transforms whom He chooses. Sometimes it seems to be the unlikeliest person, in this case, Paul, a persecutor and murderer of believers in Jesus. The Lord Jesus shows up in a person's life and makes Himself known. His transformation of the person, Paul, is evident to the persons around him. God turned evil on its head when He took Paul out of commission on the Damascus Road. Paul's zealotry to kill turned totally around toward the God appointed gift of grace in His perseverance to spread the gospel, the good news of Jesus Christ for all people. There is nothing impossible for God. His power to turn lives around is the story here in Paul's life and is the story for each of us when we come to know the giver of life, Jesus Christ.

✦

**Mystery**
God desires for each one of us to know Him.

**Power**
His power is made perfect in weakness. God takes our sin and turns us
around and makes us into His own whom He calls righteous and
blameless through the gift of His Son.

**Paradox**
Often, we think we know what God wants and how He will bring it about.
Yet, we only know what He shows us, and most often, it is only a part of His
vast and perfect plan. He is God, and there is no other.

The Power of the Resurrection in Paul's Life

# PAUL

DAY ONE - WHO IS GOD?

*God shows up in the sinner's life*

God loves each of His children, and He demonstrates it as He shows up in our lives. Jesus showed up to save sinners, you and me, from the wrath of God. No one is exempt; but through the grace of the Lord Jesus Christ, we may have the saving grace of the Lord. Jesus died for each of us to know the love of God and His provision for us now and for eternity.

You may ask why would God show up in my life? His answer is that He loves you so much that He gave up His only Son, Jesus, to death on the cross for your sake, your life and eternity with Him. We are all sinners, and there is nothing that we can do to make God love us more or less. His death on the cross was for each one of His creation. He does not want one to live without knowing Him and the saving grace He offers; He pursues each one of His creation with lovingkindness.

God shows up in the sinner's life just as He did Paul's (Saul's) on the Damascus road. God asked Paul as He blinded him, "Saul, Saul, why are you persecuting me?" Saul answered Him and called Him, "Lord." God's love toward sinners is truth, and it is present and active; in Acts 9, we see God's intervention in Saul's life. God loves the wayward; He continues to go after them. The wayward include all of us; not one of us is without sin in our lives. "All fall short of the glory of God," the scripture says. Paul says of himself that he was the worst of all sinners (1 Timothy 1:15-16).

We know that Paul recognized the voice of the Lord because he replied by calling Him "Lord." How did Paul know it was the Lord? God gave Paul the capacity to know it was He and to answer Him. God loves each one of His children, no matter who they are or what they have done. God's love requires a response. If we have none, we have rejected Him. If we say to Him "later" or "not today," we have also rejected Him. In a moment, God turned Paul's life around. God shows up to demonstrate His love toward each of us. How has God shown His love to you? Have you answered Him?

✦

> "I PRAY THAT THE EYES OF YOUR HEART MAY BE ENLIGHTENED IN ORDER THAT YOU MAY KNOW THE HOPE TO WHICH HE HAS CALLED YOU, THE RICHES OF HIS GLORIOUS INHERITANCE IN HIS HOLY PEOPLE, AND HIS INCOMPARABLY GREAT POWER FOR US WHO BELIEVE. THAT POWER IS THE SAME AS THE MIGHTY STRENGTH HE EXERTED WHEN HE RAISED CHRIST FROM THE DEAD AND SEATED HIM AT HIS RIGHT HAND IN THE HEAVENLY REALMS ..." - EPHESIANS 1:18-20

**Read Acts 9:1-31**
In this first segment, who is God?

# PAUL

DAY ONE - WHO IS GOD?

# PAUL

DAY TWO - WHAT IS THE DILEMMA?

*With His lovingkindness, God works to transform the life of His child*

God's love is transforming. Saul's life was never the same after His encounter with the risen Lord. The change was not only external, but internal and also eternal; his blindness on the Damascus Road catapulted Saul, now Paul, into real sight and knowledge of the Lord Jesus Christ.

God's grace extended to Saul and to each of us is not paralleled by anything else. When received as it was by Paul, it is life changing. God gives with it not only salvation from sin but purpose in this life which was ordained by God before the creation of the world. Paul had lived as a persecutor and murderer of Christians and was on his way to do more damage when God stopped him in his tracks on the road to Damascus. Has God stopped you from something or intervened in a way that was life changing? How has God shown you His love through it?

Jesus never tires of loving us. The grace of God does not get old; it is always fresh and new. We may miss it, however, and in doing so, not receive what God has intended for us. We get tired and weary and miss the grace of God in the moment. Grace may be in the form of a trial or suffering. We often think that following the Lord precludes the bad things in life. In order to receive the grace extended to us, we will suffer. Jesus came to give the ultimate gift of grace, suffering unto death so that we may have life eternal with Him; there is no gift with which to compare. Jesus comes to us in suffering. Jesus came to Paul and became not only His Savior, but also his life through hardship and suffering while sharing the gospel message of Jesus.

Paul knew the fullness of God through what he suffered. Jesus came to give us the fullness of God; He did it once and for all. May we receive it in full.

✦

> "I BECAME A SERVANT OF THE GOSPEL BY THE GIFT OF GOD'S GRACE GIVEN ME BY THE WORKING OF HIS POWER." - EPHESIANS 3:7

**Read Acts 13-15, 16-18, 19-20**

In this second segment, what is the dilemma? In Paul's life and travels? In His work and preaching?

# PAUL

DAY TWO - WHAT IS THE DILEMMA?

# PAUL

DAY THREE - WHAT IS GOD'S RESCUE?

*God comes to rescue us to Himself and to give us more than we imagine*

God comes to rescue us sinners from ourselves. He also comes to rescue us to Himself. Saul needed to be rescued as does each one of us. God not only saved Saul, now Paul, but He also gave him the ability to receive the rescue. Each of us has to decide if we want to be rescued or if we want to keep on living as we are. Our stubborn nature keeps us from the very thing that will free us from becoming who God created us to be if we do not say "yes" to the One who can deliver us from ourselves.

Paul not only received God's grace in Jesus Christ, but he also became a proclaimer of the gospel. God's plans for Paul included much grace and a purpose for his life that Paul would never have imagined. As Paul endured much suffering and persecution for the calling from God for His people, Paul knew and relied upon the Savior, Jesus. Paul knew that all that came in his life was known by Him. In Philippians 3:10, Paul states that in order to know Him, we join in suffering even as Jesus did in death. To know Jesus is to know grace and suffering.

God's arm of salvation came through Jesus on the cross who rose to give us new life in Him. The Holy Spirit enabled Paul to live for Christ and to consider that death would be gain if he were to be with Jesus sooner. With the Holy Spirit's guidance, Paul traveled throughout Europe and Asia to spread the gospel. Sometimes, the Holy Spirit kept him from going places; at other times, Paul, led by the Holy Spirit, traveled far and wide. Paul knew hard times, hunger, persecution, beatings, imprisonment, and even being shipwrecked.

Paul knew grace in countless ways and preached often of the boundless grace of God. He called himself the worst of all sinners who was given by God a gift to preach the good news. God's grace continues throughout our lives. His lovingkindness never ends. Do you know the grace of God in Jesus Christ? Have you received it?

✦

> "I PRAY OUT OF HIS GLORIOUS RICHES HE MAY STRENGTHEN YOU WITH POWER THROUGH HIS SPIRIT IN YOUR INNER BEING..." - EPHESIANS 3:16

**Read Philippians 1-4**
In this third segment, what is God's rescue for Paul? And for us?

# PAUL

DAY THREE - WHAT IS GOD'S RESCUE?

# PAUL

DAY FOUR - WHAT IS THE RESULT OF GOD'S RESCUE?

*God gives us as His children the ability to receive His grace and live the new life as His child*

Jesus is the grace of God to us. After meeting Jesus, Paul was never the same. His old life full of hate and persecution of Christians and death to Christianity was over. His new life is visible through his life's story and his letters in scripture. Driven by the grace of God, he not only sees himself as a sinner saved by grace, he also wants everyone he meets to know and experience life to the full in Jesus Christ.

Paul's letters describe God's love for each of us and the gift that He has given us in Jesus Christ. His description of a child of God and the blessings of heirs of Christ Jesus give us God's perspective and what God sees as He looks at us; he also illustrates the full and complete blessings we have as followers of Jesus and ones who bear His name.

Paul knew who he was and to whom he belonged. His life became a living testimony for Jesus. At first the disciples and the apostles could not trust what Paul was doing and saying, but after a short while, they knew that what had happened in his life was a transformation only God could make. Paul received the new life and was living proof of it. What is in the way of your receiving fully what Jesus has given? Do you know to whom you belong and what that means? If you wrote a description of who you are, what would it include? Paul wrote and preached the good news. He lived it with fervor in the Holy Spirit. Jesus died once and for all; new life is a gift to receive and live. Have you received it in full?

---

> "(YOU) MAY HAVE POWER, TOGETHER WITH ALL THE LORD'S HOLY PEOPLE, TO GRASP HOW WIDE AND LONG AND HIGH AND DEEP IS THE LOVE OF CHRIST AND TO KNOW THAT THIS LOVE SURPASSES KNOWLEDGE THAT YOU MAY BE FILLED TO THE MEASURE OF ALL THE FULLNESS OF GOD" - EPHESIANS 3:18-19

### Read Ephesians 1-6
In this fourth segment, what is the result of God's rescue? And for us?

# PAUL

DAY FOUR - WHAT IS THE RESULT OF GOD'S RESCUE?

# PAUL

DAY FIVE - WHAT IS THE "STORY FOR GOD'S GLORY?"

*God's desire is for each child of His to live life to the full and to ask Him for it*

God knew the heart of Saul as a sinner and also knew the heart of the man God created Saul to be in Paul. God chose Paul to receive the boundless grace of Jesus. He wants that for each of us too. God confronts us with the truth of who He is. As Paul faced his own depravity and realized that he could not live without Christ, Paul received the riches lavished upon him in Jesus. Have we faced our sinful hearts and ways, and have we embraced the magnitude of the gift of grace, not deserved, in Jesus, and not earned by anything we have done?

God wants us to have Him in full measure. What does this mean? He wants us to have all of what He has given, to know Jesus and receive His blessings and promises fully. Paul's life became one of fullness —knowing Him through joy, sorrow, suffering, and pain. He lived as if it were his last day every day. God gave him the capacity to live like this daily. We have already been given that which will enable us to live with fervor for His purposes. As we take hold of this knowledge and lean in to live it, God through the Holy Spirit encourages us and gives us the wherewithal to do it. Paul knew these things. It was not only that he saw himself as chief of sinners that he experienced grace wholeheartedly, it was also that he knew the One who gave it. Paul embraced the Giver of all that is good, holy, right, just, loving, and kind. He looked up and saw the righteous right hand of the Savior; he looked in front of him and knew that the Lord was with him and going before him wherever he went. He saw that there was nothing that God would not do for him or for any of his children, because God in Jesus Christ had already done the hardest and the greatest. It was done. He is the One and Only for whom we yearn and seek.

God uses whom He chooses for His purposes. He has a purpose for your life, and it will require that you have the fullness of Christ Jesus. May we ask Him to help us receive all that He has fully given. Embracing the full measure whether through joy, sorrow, suffering, and pain, may we live to know Him.

---

> **"FINALLY, BE STRONG IN THE LORD AND IN HIS MIGHTY POWER." - EPHESIANS 6:10**

**Read Ephesians 3**
What is the story for God's glory in Paul's life? How does Paul describe what the Lord has done for Him and for all of us?

# PAUL

DAY FIVE - WHAT IS THE "STORY FOR GOD'S GLORY?"

# PAUL

DAY SIX - WHAT ARE GOD'S TRUTHS?

*Trusting God with our broken places*

God gives grace to us freely, including the ability to receive the grace He gives. Paul received the grace of the Lord and became a proclaimer of the gospel news in Jesus Christ. God gave him the ability to surrender everything to serve the living Lord.

Paul referred to himself as the worst of all sinners. Each of us in our heart of hearts before God reflects on our gravest sins against God. In God's tender embrace we release them back to Him; He has already covered them in Jesus. While we know we are sinners of the worst kind, He comes for this reason to rescue each of us to Himself. He gives us the means to come, the wherewithal to receive His embrace, and capacity to walk with Him on this earth and for eternity. These things were real to Paul. He meant it when he said that he was the worst of sinners; he had persecuted and murdered the friends and followers of Jesus Christ. Who better to serve Jesus than one who knew God's forgiveness and the new life in Jesus? Jesus knows our hearts just as He did Paul's; what He gives us when we receive it becomes the very thing that makes us step out and continue to follow Him as grace recipients who want the world to know Him. The world will know Him through our privilege of serving Him. Paul is the perfect testimony of this truth; God transforms the sinner's life into a vessel bearing the grace and truth of Jesus.

What is difficult for me to surrender? The mountain that is I in the way of God's best, God's grace for the broken places within me, no matter how big they are.

✦

> "BUT WHEN HE, THE SPIRIT OF TRUTH, COMES, HE WILL GUIDE YOU INTO ALL THE TRUTH"
> - JOHN 16:13A

### Reflections

In this sixth segment, what are God's truths which you have learned from Paul's story and life? Describe God's gift of faith to Paul in his broken places? Have you trusted God in your brokenness?

# PAUL

DAY SIX - WHAT ARE GOD'S TRUTHS?

# A PERSPECTIVE
HOW GOD BECOMES THE MAIN CHARACTER OF OUR STORIES

If we start with "Who is He?" or "What is He up to?" we may not know the answer but we will have our eyes, hearts, and ears pointed in the right direction. We may look for how God is using this situation or circumstance in our lives or others around us. Who is God in this situation?

Often, we do not start out with this perspective. We are suffering and want to know why God is allowing it in my life. We don't want to suffer. Yet, God in His faithfulness is present. He promises that He will never leave us or forsake us. The scripture tells us that God provides, and His purposes will not be thwarted.

What is God up to? He is working His purposes out. In each of us. For His glory. We lose sight of this in our misery. It is in this time of need that God is offering us more of Himself. We already have all of Him in Jesus, but we have not taken hold of it. It is through the suffering that we may take hold of Him. He becomes more to us. We become less. Living it out in the suffering is the means God uses to transform us and make us more dependent as He gives us a more intimate relationship with Him. Our view of Him changes because He is changing us. God becomes the main character of the story of our lives as we become more dependent on Him. It is through this vital part of our story within God's great one that we become the lesser part and He becomes the larger.

As Moses told the Israelites, "He is your life." God becomes our life. He is the main in the story that He has written for us. We are His plan A from the beginning. He loved us so much that He meets us where we are and gives us Himself for a wild and wonderful story for such a time as this for the world to know Him. He becomes our story. Mary Magdalene has a similar encounter with the Lord. She does not expect to see Him because she is mourning that He is not in the tomb where He was laid after the crucifixion. When Jesus asks her in the garden for whom she was looking and then calls her by name, she knows that she has seen the Lord. She runs to tell the other disciples, "I have seen the Lord!" Jesus calls us by name. He makes Himself known to us. We see the Lord. He is our life.

Isaiah 45:3 says, "I will give you treasures of darkness, riches stored in secret places, so that you may know the Lord, the God of Israel, who summons you by name." Is He summoning you now? Are you in the midst of something really difficult and there is no place to go except into His arms? His love beckons us to come, and His treasure and riches are the counterpart to any difficulty or need that we may have. We are His children, and He calls us by name. We know that it is He, the Lord.

Is God the main character in your story? Do you want Him to be?

PART VII

# MOSES

THE LORD IS "YOUR LIFE"

MORE OF GOD IN OUR LIVES AND STORIES

THIS DAY I CALL THE HEAVENS AND
THE EARTH AS WITNESSES AGAINST
YOU THAT I HAVE SET BEFORE YOU
LIFE AND DEATH, BLESSINGS AND
CURSES. NOW CHOOSE LIFE, SO
THAT YOU AND YOUR CHILDREN
MAY LIVE AND THAT YOU MAY
LOVE THE LORD YOUR GOD, LISTEN
TO HIS VOICE, AND HOLD FAST TO
HIM. FOR THE LORD IS YOUR LIFE,
AND HE WILL GIVE YOU MANY
YEARS IN THE LAND HE SWORE TO
GIVE TO YOUR FATHERS, ABRAHAM,
ISAAC AND JACOB.

DEUTERONOMY 30:19-20

## PART VII

# MOSES

THE LORD IS "YOUR LIFE"

It is fitting that we start the second half of this study with Moses; he was God's choice to lead the Israelites out of slavery and into the Promised Land of their ancestors. He is the most well-known of all Biblical persons. God imparted to Moses the ability to have a relationship with Him, the High, Exalted, and Holy God of the universe, in ways He had not done with any other person before him.

Moses received the leadership of God's people tentatively; however, God used him mightily. It says in Deuteronomy that no prophet has risen in Israel like Moses, whom the Lord knew face to face and who performed the awesome deeds of the Lord in the sight of Israel. Yet, Moses erred just like any other human being does; the Lord withheld from him entry into the Promised Land. The Israelites approached and entered the land under Joshua's rule.

God chose exactly who He intended to lead His people: Moses, who grew up in the house of Pharaoh and watched his people be abused as slaves. There was a time when Moses left Pharaoh's house after he murdered a fellow Egyptian who had harmed a Hebrew slave. God uses all of our experiences as He did with Moses to lead the life of God's purposes for Him and for His people.

✦

**Mystery**
Moses, a human being like you and me, was used for
the glory of God for His purposes.

**Power**
God, who is holy, comes down to us to be in relationship with us.

**Paradox**
God's power displayed in the life of Moses becomes the power by which
the world knows Him.

# MOSES

DAY ONE - WHO IS GOD?

*God invites us to know Him*

God shows up in His child's life, Moses. God comes to Moses in a burning bush and invites Him into His presence. Moses fears the Lord and is also afraid to do what He has instructed him to do. Yet, God calls Moses. God chooses Moses to lead His people out of slavery and oppression by Pharaoh and the Egyptians. God says that He has heard the cries of His people and has come to free them through Moses going to Pharaoh. When Moses asks the Lord who He would say He is, the Lord replies, "I AM who I AM." God intervenes in Moses' life just as He does ours. The Lord comes into our lives to show us Himself. He wants us to know Him, to have a relationship with Him. God gives us the capacity to revere Him and to draw near as He draws near to us.

God invites us onto holy ground as He comes into our lives; He is holy ground to be revered and honored and worshipped. Yet, He comes to us in all of our depravity. Moses met Him as he approached the burning bush to see what was going on with a bush that would not be consumed by the fire. Throughout the life of Moses, God met with him to give him instruction as to how to lead the Israelites. Moses would return to the people with an afterglow from meeting with his Holy Father God; no one has since met with God as Moses did. God's invitation and gift to know Him in Jesus Christ is greater than anything we can fathom.

Whenever we hear His voice, He invites us to enter in with Him. He is God; there is no other. Imagine that the great God of the universe has invited you to come meet with Him. There is no better invitation we will ever receive. What is your response?

✦

> "I PRAY THAT THE EYES OF YOUR HEART MAY BE ENLIGHTENED IN ORDER THAT YOU MAY KNOW THE HOPE TO WHICH HE HAS CALLED YOU, THE RICHES OF HIS GLORIOUS INHERITANCE IN HIS HOLY PEOPLE, AND HIS INCOMPARABLY GREAT POWER FOR US WHO BELIEVE. THAT POWER IS THE SAME AS THE MIGHTY STRENGTH HE EXERTED WHEN HE RAISED CHRIST FROM THE DEAD AND SEATED HIM AT HIS RIGHT HAND IN THE HEAVENLY REALMS ..." - EPHESIANS 1:18-20

**Read Exodus 3-5; Isaiah 61**
In this first segment, who is God? How does He show His presence?

The Lord is "Your Life"

# MOSES

DAY ONE - WHO IS GOD?

The Power of the Resurrection in Moses's Life

# MOSES

DAY TWO - WHAT IS THE DILEMMA?

*God never tires of guiding, leading, and pursuing His own*

In this story of Moses' encounter with the Living Lord, we see God's intervention, His intentional invitation to Moses, not only for the sake of Moses but also for the sake of all the Israelites. The invitation to holy ground is also a personal introduction to the great God of all the earth, the One who knows and sees and enters in with compassion and love. God demonstrates His love to Moses by hearing their pleas and reminding them that He is with them and is here to rescue them.

God shows us His love through His presence and His hearing and answering our cries for help. He answers before we call. God is always with us and will never leave us. His love, which is the same yesterday, today, and forever, continues to run after us, hold us, and rescue us. Moses and the Israelites needed His rescue. God guided the Israelites through the desert under Moses' leadership, His rescue plan for them. He gave them the means to gather as a community and worship Him with the design and building of the tabernacle, all manner of provision for them in the wilderness.

God also showed up in Moses' life as the rescuer. He never tires of hearing our cries. From our tears of our weakest and darkest moments to the hallelujahs for the answers from our great God, we need Him. God knows our needs without our telling Him, but as we see in Moses' story, God seeks out a relationship with His child, Moses. He is also pursuing each of us for a relationship with Him. What is your answer to His running after you? Will you enter in with Him? It is holy ground.

✦

> "I BECAME A SERVANT OF THE GOSPEL BY THE GIFT OF GOD'S GRACE GIVEN ME BY THE WORKING OF HIS POWER." - EPHESIANS 3:7

**Read Exodus 6:1-12; Isaiah 57:15; Deuteronomy 30:19-20**
What is the dilemma in these scripture passages? What is the dilemma for Moses? For us?

# MOSES

DAY TWO - WHAT IS THE DILEMMA?

# MOSES

DAY THREE - WHAT IS GOD'S RESCUE?

*God's timing is perfect*

God's rescue is always on target, on time, and precise in every detail. This is the character of God; He cannot be anything less. The great story of the exodus of God's people out of the slavery of the Egyptians is one for the ages, and it all began with Moses' encounter with God in the burning bush. Actually, it began in the heart of God before creation, but the story in the text started in this encounter.

Moses was reverent before God, and he also feared what God wanted him to do. God gives the capacity to fear Him, to be in awe and to humbly approach Him, and the wherewithal to follow through with His instructions; neither are we able to do on our own. The conversation ensues, and God continues to show Moses who He is; God's answers contain beautiful illustrations of not only who He is and what He does but also who we are as we follow Him. Knowing Him and His presence for and with us are the keys to our identity as His children. God already knew Moses' heart and questions; yet, God answers with assurances.

God met Moses in the wilderness to invite Moses to know Him. God is issuing you an invitation. His timing is perfect in every detail. He knows you and wants you to know Him. Are you willing to enter in?

✦

> "I PRAY OUT OF HIS GLORIOUS RICHES HE MAY STRENGTHEN YOU WITH POWER THROUGH HIS SPIRIT IN YOUR INNER BEING..." - EPHESIANS 3:16

**Read Exodus 6:1-8**
What is God's rescue? What is God's rescue for Moses? For the Israelites?

The Lord is "Your Life"

# MOSES

DAY THREE - WHAT IS GOD'S RESCUE?

# MOSES

DAY FOUR - WHAT IS THE RESULT OF GOD'S RESCUE?

*God knows our strengths and our weaknesses and determines the length of our days*

The Israelites cried out to God in their misery under the abusive treatment of the Egyptians. God heard them and answered. He hears us too even before we call on Him. God lets us know that He hears us and desires to rescue us. He came to Moses and told him that He heard their cry. Moses in his earlier days had been part of both cultures; he knew the abuse as a Hebrew slave and as one under the protection of the Pharaoh. He had grown up being protected by his own mother as she put him in a basket in the Nile only for Pharaoh's daughter to retrieve him and rear him as her own. Understanding the plight of the Hebrews, being one himself to being part of Pharaoh's household, Moses retreated to the wilderness after murdering an abusive Egyptian of a Hebrew slave. God intervened for all the Israelites' sake.

Moses knew his vulnerabilities, his sin, and runs away to the wilderness. But God does not leave him there. Neither does He leave us to our own devices. He enters in with us. We must determine if we will enter in with Him. God created each of us for a purpose, one for the world to know Him. He knows our every sin and flaw, and yet, uses them for His great purposes when we decide to choose Him and His ways. God invites Moses to a new call, God's call for his life.

✦

> "(YOU) MAY HAVE POWER, TOGETHER WITH ALL THE LORD'S HOLY PEOPLE, TO GRASP HOW WIDE AND LONG AND HIGH AND DEEP IS THE LOVE OF CHRIST AND TO KNOW THAT THIS LOVE SURPASSES KNOWLEDGE THAT YOU MAY BE FILLED TO THE MEASURE OF ALL THE FULLNESS OF GOD" - EPHESIANS 3:18-19

**Read Exodus 2; Exodus 6:28-7:13**
What is the result of God's rescue? For Moses and the Israelites?

# MOSES

DAY FOUR - WHAT IS THE RESULT OF GOD'S RESCUE?

The Power of the Resurrection in Moses's Life

# MOSES

DAY FIVE - WHAT IS THE "STORY FOR GOD'S GLORY?"

*God knows us and longs to show us His glory and when He does, it is more than we can behold*

Sometimes we long to see the whole and the answers and all that is ahead, but God knows that we are not able to because it is too much for us to see and grasp. The same is true of God's likeness, His glory, His character displayed for us to see. We cannot behold it; it is overwhelmingly more than we are able to take in. However, God gives us glimpses along the way. Moses entered into a relationship with the Living Lord, and it was good, challenging, and totally worth it.

After the crossing of the Red Sea and the deliverance from slavery, Moses led the Israelites. As the Israelites moved through the desert, God guided them and taught them. He provided what they needed daily. It was the Lord who led them, fed them, and kept them safe; Moses knew this because he communed with Him. Through a personal relationship with the Lord, Moses was able to know Him in ways that he never thought possible. Do you yearn for more?

God through Moses instructs us to choose life and God's blessings over death and cursings. He says to us that He is the Lord our God whom we are to love, to listen to His voice, and to hold fast to Him. He is our life. Choose Him. God chose Moses, and He chooses each of us to love Him, to listen to Him, and to hold fast to Him, because He is our life. (Deuteronomy 30:19-20) Are we going to choose Him, the Life?

✦

> "FINALLY, BE STRONG IN THE LORD AND IN HIS MIGHTY POWER." - EPHESIANS 6:10

**Read Exodus 12:31-15; Psalm 90**
What is the "story for God's glory?" What does Moses write about God's story in their lives in Psalm 90?

The Lord is "Your Life"

# MOSES

DAY FIVE - WHAT IS THE "STORY FOR GOD'S GLORY?"

The Power of the Resurrection in Moses's Life

# MOSES

DAY SIX - WHAT ARE GOD'S TRUTHS?

*Trusting God personally in relationship*

God wanted a relationship with Moses. He chooses whom He chooses. What an amazing gift! A relationship with the living Lord. Moses became a confidante of the Lord because the Lord made it so. It was personal, and it was holy. It is what the Lord wants for each of us in Jesus Christ.

Moses was wandering in the desert when God came to him and called him to go to Pharaoh to release the Israelites from their enslavement. God not only confronts Moses with this task but He gives Moses the honor of being in relationship with Him. Do we know the truth about a relationship with the Living Lord?

Moses began talking with the Lord. Actually, Moses said that he was not up to what the Lord was asking him to do. Yet, the Lord pursued the conversation and gave him what he asked: one to help him, Aaron. This relationship included conversation which is what God chose to have with Moses. God created the relationship, and He has also chosen it for us. We see this in Moses' interactions with God. He asks the Lord for His favor, His presence, and to go with him. God enabled Moses to talk with Him; He enables us to talk with Him too.

What is more important than this relationship in our lives? If we are lacking in anything, the Lord is the answer. Where am I wandering? God is near. May we know His favor and presence and guidance in all things. I do not even have to ask, except that He longs for me to converse with Him. He delights in rescuing me and showing me His ways and thoughts just as He did with Moses.

✦

> "BUT WHEN HE, THE SPIRIT OF TRUTH, COMES, HE WILL GUIDE YOU INTO ALL THE TRUTH" - JOHN 16:13A

**Reflect on the truths of God from Moses' life.**
What are the truths of God you have learned from Moses' story and from your own?
Who was God to Moses? How did He become so to Moses? Who is He to you?

The Lord is "Your Life"

# MOSES

DAY SIX - WHAT ARE GOD'S TRUTHS?

# A PERSPECTIVE
## PRAYING

The relationship with the Lord grows deeper with prayer: listening and conversing with God about all of life. Nothing is too small for God; neither is anything too hard for Him. One thing one knows if one has been a follower of Jesus for a while is that prayer is for the long haul. It also takes the long view. God wants a relationship with us, and in fact, we were wired to want one with Him above all else.

God knows our hearts and minds and knows our prayers before we utter them. He also knows our groanings. He is deeply concerned and never leaves us. He is answering before we call out to Him. Through the power of the Holy Spirit, we have the means to go to God in prayer and seek Him and to ask Him for all things. After we have done so, we may know that He has heard us and that He will answer. We can rest that the sovereign Lord of the universe has the prayer and will answer in our best interests. This too is a gift from God: the ability to trust that He has it. During our conversing, listening to Him in His word, worshipping Him, and interceding on others' behalf and our own, our capacity for prayer grows. God multiplies our small steps of faith. Leaning all into our Lord and Savior for all that we ask or imagine becomes a daily process, one in which we change and grow in depending on Him. He never gives up on us, and we come to know His heart for us is so large we cannot fathom it. He knows our deepest hurts and our highest dreams and wants to listen to our hearts at all times.

*Waiting in prayer*
Waiting is not easy, especially if our focus is on the thing for which we are waiting instead of on God. Continuing to fix our eyes on God is key. It is during this daily process of walking and talking with God that He shows us who He is and what He does. He gives us His best as we attempt this new life in Him. As we know Him, the Holy Spirit gives us the capacity to wait, to ask the King of Glory who He is in this circumstance, and to know His heart and way with us. Time is His; yet, He uses it to prepare us, to grow us up, and to receive more and more of the fullness of Jesus Christ. It may seem that there has been an interruption in the plan of one's life. Waiting seems long, but God's purposes are not thwarted. He is up to something, something big.

✦

Things to know in the waiting:

- Live large today. God has given you the kingdom.
- Jesus is a mighty warrior and a gentle shepherd; nothing is too small or too difficult for Him.
- Pray to have a thirst for God.
- Expect more of God in your life. Ask to be hungry, thirsty, to yearn, to long, and to dream big.
- Examine the heart for walled off places or barriers to relationship or places of hurt to be healed.
- Empty one's self of self, the past, and of critical analysis.
- Ask Him for a pure heart, to forgive, and to have compassion.
- Collaborate with God to move forward with small steps of faith.
- Trust Him and who He is and for who you are and for your journey each moment of each day.

Would you ask the Lord for a heart of prayer? Journal your thoughts. You may write your prayer if you would like in the space below.

PART VII

# MARY MAGDALENE

HE IS RISEN

MORE OF GOD IN OUR LIVES AND STORIES

WHEN JESUS ROSE EARLY ON THE FIRST DAY OF THE WEEK, HE APPEARED FIRST TO MARY MAGDALENE, OUT OF WHOM HE HAD DRIVEN SEVEN DEMONS. SHE WENT AND TOLD THOSE WHO HAD BEEN WITH HIM AND WHO WERE MOURNING AND WEEPING. WHEN THEY HEARD THAT JESUS WAS ALIVE AND THAT SHE HAD SEEN HIM, THEY DID NOT BELIEVE IT.

MARK 16:9-11

## PART VIII
# MARY MAGDALENE
#### HE IS RISEN

Mary Magdalene was an unlikely disciple of Jesus; yet, she was truly one of His beloved, who followed Him and believed Him with her whole heart. I guess you could say all of us are unlikely candidates. But Mary Magdalene had a couple of things that made her less probable for the role of disciple: first, she was a woman in her day, and secondly, she was once possessed by demons. Neither of these things stopped Jesus from choosing her.

We can be encouraged by Jesus' choosing of His own; He chooses whom He chooses, and they look like us. Mary Magdalene was the first to share the news of Jesus' resurrection. What an honor and privilege in front of the world to be able to shout that her Savior had risen! Do we feel this way when we share our hope in Jesus? It is a privilege!

✦

**Mystery**
Sharing the news of the Savior is what He calls us to do. First though,
He gives us the means to believe Him ourselves, and then,
He equips us to spread the gospel.

**Power**
Jesus uses sinners, for whom He died, for His purposes.

**Paradox**
Jesus always talked about our work on earth is to believe the One the Lord
sent. He gives us the capacity to believe. It is by this power that we are His
own.

The Power of the Resurrection in Mary Magdalene's Life

# MARY MAGDALENE

DAY ONE - WHO IS GOD?

*Jesus comes to comfort and to heal us*

Jesus is the healer who sees and knows our greatest needs and struggles. He knows our secret addictions, financial woes, things we keep to ourselves not even shared with our spouses, and mental illness. As we wait in silence for a remedy, the world seems lonely and unbearable. Mary Magdalene knew this kind of pain; she was possessed by seven demons. Jesus healed her. He comes to comfort and to heal us from our brokenness of all kinds, shapes, and sizes. As a woman in her day and culture and a condition of this kind, Mary Magdalene was in dire straits. Yet, Jesus comes. He comes for each of us in our pain and struggles, even when we do not know how badly we need Him.

It could be said that the severity of Mary Magdalene's condition led to her great gratitude, and I believe that this is true. It is also true that as we come to know Jesus and His great love for us, we are humbled and awed at the gravity of our sin before Him. Jesus gives us the capacity for receiving the knowledge of Him and His great grace. Mary Magdalene grasped the healing He gave her because she received the Giver just as she received His healing. Knowing Jesus is the life.

May we recognize our deep need for Jesus. May we know Him as we receive His comfort and healing.

✦

> "I PRAY THAT THE EYES OF YOUR HEART MAY BE ENLIGHTENED IN ORDER THAT YOU MAY KNOW THE HOPE TO WHICH HE HAS CALLED YOU, THE RICHES OF HIS GLORIOUS INHERITANCE IN HIS HOLY PEOPLE, AND HIS INCOMPARABLY GREAT POWER FOR US WHO BELIEVE. THAT POWER IS THE SAME AS THE MIGHTY STRENGTH HE EXERTED WHEN HE RAISED CHRIST FROM THE DEAD AND SEATED HIM AT HIS RIGHT HAND IN THE HEAVENLY REALMS ..." - EPHESIANS 1:18-20

**Read Mark 16:9; Psalm 27**
Who is God? Who is He is these scripture passages?

# MARY MAGDALENE

DAY ONE - WHO IS GOD?

# MARY MAGDALENE

DAY TWO - WHAT IS THE DILEMMA?

*Jesus gives us new life and a story to go with it*

Jesus chose Mary Magdalene to be His disciple; she is one of the few women named as disciples of Jesus in scripture. Her healing was the great impetus in her life to share the news of the gospel of Jesus Christ. She came to the tomb to tend to the body of Jesus to find the stone rolled away and His body missing. She was a disciple and friend, a follower of Jesus, and a woman who knew her Savior. It was devastating to lose Him, to see him die such a horrific death. In her sorrow, she wept.

As Jesus answered her and she realized that it was not the gardener, but Jesus, she hugged Him and held onto Him. He told her to let Him go and to go tell the others about what she had seen, that He is alive. It is not an accident that Mary Magdalene was the one who found Jesus alive; God planned each detail of His only Son's death and resurrection.

Mary Magdalene had the privilege of announcing Jesus' resurrection from the dead. He is risen! Jesus is risen indeed. We experience it again and again if we walk in faith with Him. Jesus gave her new life with her healing, and He gives it once again as she sees Him at the empty tomb. Who is this Jesus who rose again from the tomb? As part of her story, Mary Magdalene has the honor of sharing the news of her Savior's resurrection. It was not only His, but hers. And that is the way it works for each of us as Jesus' followers. In His resurrection, He gives us new life and with it He gives us a story to tell, ours, in His greater one. Have you experienced new life in Jesus? What is your story?

✦

> "I BECAME A SERVANT OF THE GOSPEL BY THE GIFT OF GOD'S GRACE GIVEN ME BY THE WORKING OF HIS POWER." - EPHESIANS 3:7

**Read Mark 16:9-11; John 20:11-18**
What is the dilemma?

# MARY MAGDALENE
DAY TWO - WHAT IS THE DILEMMA?

# MARY MAGDALENE

DAY THREE - WHAT IS GOD'S RESCUE?

*Jesus is the One we seek*

Have we acknowledged that we are searching for something or someone in this life? Perhaps life seems full, maybe not perfect, but plenty busy and challenging and mostly good. But it doesn't stay this way. This is not pessimism, but a fact of life. We were created with a deep cavity which we tend to fill with things that we dream about, things we want in life, aspirations, friends and family, and worldly stuff. However, God has a better plan for each of us. When we reach the end of ourselves and our need to fill this chasm within, it is a good thing. Out of our deep need comes the cry of our hearts for God Himself; we may not know it or even want to realize it, but this is true.

Jesus meets our deepest need. He is waiting for each of us to call on Him. He is the One we seek, the desire of our hearts. The Creator Himself comes in Jesus Christ to be our Savior, to rescue us from ourselves, and to be with us in this life. Only He can fill the deep chasm within us.

When Mary Magdalene realized her Jesus was gone, even His body, she was grief-stricken. Her understanding of Jesus was limited to her human perspective of His life and death. It is this way for us too. We cannot understand the ways of God, but He can reveal Himself to us. As we cry out to Him, He answers and reveals Himself in ways we are not expecting.

May we hope in Him, expect His presence, and live in awe of it as we choose to follow Him and come to know Him, the One and Only we seek.

✦

> "I PRAY OUT OF HIS GLORIOUS RICHES HE MAY STRENGTHEN YOU WITH POWER THROUGH HIS SPIRIT IN YOUR INNER BEING..." -EPHESIANS 3:16

**Read Isaiah 51:1-16; John 20:11-18**
What is God's rescue?

# MARY MAGDALENE

DAY THREE - WHAT IS GOD'S RESCUE?

# MARY MAGDALENE

DAY FOUR - WHAT IS THE RESULT OF GOD'S RESCUE?

*Jesus presents Himself to us and gives us the ability to see and know Him*

We do not have the capability to love Jesus as He loves us. Only He can give us this too. Jesus extends His arm, takes us in, and then surrounds us and enables us to receive the love He has already given. In addition, He opens our eyes to see Him, our ears to hear His voice, and our hearts to know Him.

He compares His role to that of a shepherd whose voice the sheep know. Jesus' voice is one we know if we follow Him. He envelops us in His grace and protects us from the things that would ensnare us. In addition, He leads us out into the world; He goes before us, with us, and after us. (John 10)

Mary Magdalene knew her Shepherd, her Savior. She had lived a hard life and had experienced much pain; yet, Jesus freed her to follow Him, to receive His grace and healing, and to lead her out to be his disciple. It is the same for each of us. Jesus takes our broken places and heals them, and we all have them. He gives us the ability to receive the new life in Him and to follow Him as He leads us out each day. We know and follow Him because we know His voice, the One of our Lord and Savior, Jesus Christ.

✦

> "(YOU) MAY HAVE POWER, TOGETHER WITH ALL THE LORD'S HOLY PEOPLE, TO GRASP HOW WIDE AND LONG AND HIGH AND DEEP IS THE LOVE OF CHRIST AND TO KNOW THAT THIS LOVE SURPASSES KNOWLEDGE THAT YOU MAY BE FILLED TO THE MEASURE OF ALL THE FULLNESS OF GOD" - EPHESIANS 3:18-1

**Read John 10:4b; Psalm 34:18; John 20**
What is the result of God's rescue?

# MARY MAGDALENE

DAY FOUR - WHAT IS THE RESULT OF GOD'S RESCUE?

# MARY MAGDALENE
DAY FIVE - WHAT IS THE "STORY FOR GOD'S GLORY?"

*Jesus knows our hearts*

Jesus knows our hearts. And He gives us a chance to communicate with Him about it. Although He already knows what is on our hearts, He wants to have a conversation, a relationship with us. He asks Mary Magdalene, "Why are you crying?" In addition, He asks, "Who are you looking for?" Often in life, we cry and perhaps can't explain our tears, except that we know we are sad. God in Jesus Christ is the great comforter, the great healer, the great physician. He knew Mary Magdalene's pain; she was grieving the loss of her Savior, Friend, Healer, and Lord. Jesus knew, but He gave her a chance to open her heart to Him. Jesus also asks about her actions, for whom was she looking. Again, Jesus knows that we are looking for something to fill our void; it is He. It is only Jesus who will fill the emptiness deep within. Isn't it curious that Jesus approaches Mary Magdalene with words that are so soothing to each of us? It is His way; He approaches each of us with His lovingkindness as salve on our deepest hurts.

The picture of Mary Magdalene going to the tomb to find it empty and Jesus waiting for her in the garden is a great picture in my mind's eye of how Jesus is standing close by each of us in our darkest moments. He shows up to be with us, to comfort, to address the very depth of our souls. Jesus does these things and more; He awakens us that He is with us in the moment and for each day to come. Just like Mary Magdalene, "Oh, it's you, Jesus" is our cry too that we have been heard by the One and Only. He is still alive; He comes to us.

✦

> "FINALLY, BE STRONG IN THE LORD AND IN HIS MIGHTY POWER." - EPHESIANS 6:1

**Read John 20:11-18; Psalm 31**
What is "the story for God's glory?" How does God show us who He is in these passages?

# MARY MAGDALENE

DAY FIVE - WHAT IS THE "STORY FOR GOD'S GLORY?"

# MARY MAGDALENE

DAY SIX - WHAT ARE GOD'S TRUTHS?

*Trusting God while never being the same again*

Mary Magdalene knew Jesus and knew His healing. Her life was never the same after the healing of the demons. She followed Jesus and served Him as He ministered to the people. As she went to the empty tomb on His resurrection Sunday and instead of finding a body to be prepared, she found who she thought was the gardener. Indeed, it was the risen Jesus. Talk about life never being the same!

May we have a great awakening of knowing grace and truth as we have never experienced before. Where are you on your journey with grace and truth? Do you know that it is real? Real in Jesus Christ?

Not only is Jesus the great healer but He is also the One who changes everything. I am no longer trapped in my life of self-driven pursuits, but I am free to be who God created me to be. Instead of living in this world of striving, achievement, pleasing, and collecting things and other, I have new life of walking with Him and serving with Him. Do I doubt that Jesus is the great Physician, the Healer of things spiritual, emotional, physical? The Lord is risen indeed.

✦

> "BUT WHEN HE, THE SPIRIT OF TRUTH, COMES, HE WILL GUIDE YOU INTO ALL THE TRUTH" - JOHN 16:13A

**Reflect on the truths of God you learned from Mary Magdalene's life.**
What happens in Mary Magdalene's life? Who was God to Mary Magdalene?
What has your story of God been so far? Who is He to you?

# MARY MAGDALENE
DAY SIX - WHAT ARE GOD'S TRUTHS?

# A PERSPECTIVE

COLLABORATION WITH GOD

Crossing over the threshold of the old way to the new is the walk of faith. We must leave a piece of ourselves behind as we crossover into the new. It may be laying down something that has been a huge part of one's life. But God. He knows all, and He requires that we let go of all else and lean into Him and hold onto Him. He will do the rest; He holds onto us and never lets us go when we decide to follow Him.

Holding all things loosely is difficult because we have people, places, dreams, and things that are lovely and good and gifts from God. Yet, God wants our surrender. Suffering is like this. We want something else, less difficult or painful. We don't want to lose our family or friends or even pieces of ourselves. In order to know God and to have all that He has intended for us, He says that we must die to ourselves, die to this life in order to gain life, life with Him eternally. Suffering means dying to self, and suffering brings about the dependency on God, truly leaning into Him as we let go and He holds onto us. It is just as it was with our forefathers in the faith; suffering was a part of their walk with God. It is in the suffering that they had fuller and richer lives with God.

✦

Are you leaning all into God?

When have you let go of something big in your life? Were you leaning into God?

What does "crossing over" into the new God has for you mean to you?

Are you willing to let go of things the Lord has asked of you?

Do you believe that God will help you move into the new?

What have you experienced in your relationship with God through suffering?

Would you say that you have "crossed over?"

PART IX

# JOSHUA

GOD FULFILLS HIS PROMISES

MORE OF GOD IN OUR LIVES AND STORIES

JOSHUA SAID TO ALL THE PEOPLE, "THIS IS WHAT THE LORD, THE GOD OF ISRAEL, SAYS: 'LONG AGO YOUR ANCESTORS, INCLUDING TERAH THE FATHER OF ABRAHAM AND NAHOR, LIVED BEYOND THE EUPHRATES RIVER AND WORSHIPED OTHER GODS. BUT I TOOK YOUR FATHER ABRAHAM FROM THE LAND BEYOND THE EUPHRATES AND LED HIM THROUGHOUT CANAAN AND GAVE HIM MANY DESCENDANTS. I GAVE HIM ISAAC, AND TO ISAAC I GAVE JACOB AND ESAU. I ASSIGNED THE HILL COUNTRY OF SEIR TO ESAU, BUT JACOB AND HIS FAMILY WENT DOWN TO EGYPT.

"'THEN I SENT MOSES AND AARON, AND I AFFLICTED THE EGYPTIANS BY WHAT I DID THERE, AND I BROUGHT YOU OUT. WHEN I BROUGHT YOUR PEOPLE OUT OF EGYPT, YOU CAME TO THE SEA, AND THE EGYPTIANS PURSUED THEM WITH CHARIOTS AND HORSEMEN AS FAR AS THE RED SEA. BUT THEY CRIED TO THE LORD FOR HELP, AND HE PUT DARKNESS BETWEEN YOU AND THE EGYPTIANS; HE BROUGHT THE SEA OVER THEM AND COVERED THEM. YOU SAW WITH YOUR OWN EYES WHAT I DID TO THE EGYPTIANS. THEN YOU LIVED IN THE WILDERNESS FOR A LONG TIME.

"'I BROUGHT YOU TO THE LAND OF THE AMORITES WHO LIVED EAST OF THE JORDAN. THEY FOUGHT AGAINST YOU, BUT I GAVE THEM INTO YOUR HANDS. I DESTROYED THEM FROM BEFORE YOU, AND YOU TOOK POSSESSION OF THEIR LAND. WHEN BALAK SON OF ZIPPOR, THE KING OF MOAB, PREPARED TO FIGHT AGAINST ISRAEL, HE SENT FOR BALAAM, SON OF BEOR, TO PUT A CURSE ON YOU. BUT I WOULD NOT LISTEN TO BALAAM, SO HE BLESSED YOU AGAIN AND AGAIN, AND I DELIVERED YOU OUT OF HIS HAND.

"'THEN YOU CROSSED THE JORDAN AND CAME TO JERICHO. THE CITIZENS OF JERICHO FOUGHT AGAINST YOU, AS DID ALSO THE AMORITES, PERIZZITES, CANAANITES, HITTITES, GIRGASHITES, HIVITES AND JEBUSITES, BUT I GAVE THEM INTO YOUR HANDS. I SENT THE HORNET AHEAD OF YOU, WHICH DROVE THEM OUT BEFORE YOU—ALSO THE TWO AMORITE KINGS. YOU DID NOT DO IT WITH YOUR OWN SWORD AND BOW. SO I GAVE YOU A LAND ON WHICH YOU DID NOT TOIL AND CITIES YOU DID NOT BUILD; AND YOU LIVE IN THEM AND EAT FROM VINEYARDS AND OLIVE GROVES THAT YOU DID NOT PLANT.'

"NOW FEAR THE LORD AND SERVE HIM WITH ALL FAITHFULNESS. THROW AWAY THE GODS YOUR ANCESTORS WORSHIPED BEYOND THE EUPHRATES RIVER AND IN EGYPT, AND SERVE THE LORD. BUT IF SERVING THE LORD SEEMS UNDESIRABLE TO YOU, THEN CHOOSE FOR YOURSELVES THIS DAY WHOM YOU WILL SERVE, WHETHER THE GODS YOUR ANCESTORS SERVED BEYOND THE EUPHRATES, OR THE GODS OF THE AMORITES, IN WHOSE LAND YOU ARE LIVING. BUT AS FOR ME AND MY HOUSEHOLD, WE WILL SERVE THE LORD."

JOSHUA 24:2-15

## PART IX
# JOSHUA
GOD FULFILLS HIS PROMISES

The life of the leader of the Israelites as they cross into the Promised Land had to be a daunting one. God had promised them the land generations before Moses and then Joshua. It was a big move for the people and an even larger one for the one who would lead them. Joshua had observed his predecessor his entire life, and now it was expected that he fill those sandals.
Yet, God is bigger than all our fears and our plans.

God equips each one of us for the tasks He gives us. Isn't it interesting that He told Joshua to be courageous and not to fear, to know that God would never leave him or forsake him. He does the same for us. God knew Joshua's heart and mind; He also gave Joshua everything he needed to lead the people into the land He promised them through His covenant with His people.

Because we are also God's people, He promises never to leave us or to forsake us. He knows our hearts and minds and gives us the means to enter in to hard things and all things He has planned for us through the power of His Holy Spirit.

✦

**Mystery**
God comes down to us to give us His heart.

**Power**
God remains with us whether we have courage or not to stay and to lean on Him. His pursuing heart knows our frailties, and He still loves us and pursues us with His love and power.

**Paradox**
Not only do we lack the means to do things on our own,
we also do not have the means to acquire it. But God does!

The Power of the Resurrection in Joshua's Life

# JOSHUA

DAY ONE - WHO IS GOD?

*God not only shows up, but He comes to us in our greatest need,*
*sometimes whether we know it or not; He knows*

I have a suspicion that Joshua knew his need for God. Moses had just died, and he was now in charge of the task to lead the Israelites into the Promised Land. This entrance was the very thing they had been working toward for years, and Joshua was the one in the lead. It was a daunting task; people already occupied the land, which meant that they would have to go in and secure it from its occupants. Joshua grew up and assisted Moses in the days of his leadership; he knew how difficult it was to lead the people.

God says to Joshua that he was not to be afraid or discouraged because He, the Lord, would be with him. Not only would He be with him, but He also would never leave him or forsake him. This is the promise God made to Joshua, and He makes the same promise to us. The reason they are entering the Promised Land is that God had promised it to the Israelites centuries earlier; God keeps His promises always. He is not able to go back on a promise. He is God, and there is no other.

Joshua needed God in order to have a clear call on what to do to lead the people, but he also needed God personally. This new position was important for all, Joshua and His people. Only God could guide and show them the way into the Promised Land. After all, it was His promise and His fulfillment of the promise that would sustain Joshua and his people. What promise are you hanging onto? Do you know the promises of God? Do you know the Giver of these promises?

✦

> "I PRAY THAT THE EYES OF YOUR HEART MAY BE ENLIGHTENED IN ORDER THAT YOU MAY KNOW THE HOPE TO WHICH HE HAS CALLED YOU, THE RICHES OF HIS GLORIOUS INHERITANCE IN HIS HOLY PEOPLE, AND HIS INCOMPARABLY GREAT POWER FOR US WHO BELIEVE. THAT POWER IS THE SAME AS THE MIGHTY STRENGTH HE EXERTED WHEN HE RAISED CHRIST FROM THE DEAD AND SEATED HIM AT HIS RIGHT HAND IN THE HEAVENLY REALMS ..." - EPHESIANS 1:18-20

**Read Joshua 1; Exodus 17:8-16**
Who is God in these scripture passages?

# JOSHUA

DAY ONE - WHO IS GOD?

# JOSHUA

DAY TWO - WHAT IS THE DILEMMA?

*When the Lord speaks to us, we know that it is He, because He reminds of who He is*

Growing up under the leadership of Moses, Joshua knew the Lord. He was walking in the Lord's footsteps; however, the job was not going to be easy. And the Lord knew that Joshua knew it; so, when the Lord shows up and speaks to Joshua, he knew it was the Lord God, the father of Abraham, Isaac, and Jacob.

Some may think that God speaks only to our forefathers in scripture, but if we are followers of God, we know His voice. It is an amazing privilege to know the voice of God. Joshua knew the words that God was speaking to Him were true. God reminds us of what we already know of Him lest we forget what we have been taught. God reminds Joshua of who He is and what He does for His own. He goes with us and never leaves us wherever we go. God would lead them into the Promised Land just as He had promised. Is there a reminder you need right now? God speaks. He reminds us of what we know to be true; the reminder of the truth of God also reminds us of whose voice we hear.

When Joshua heard the commands of the Lord, he may have had doubts about it. Perhaps, he feared that they were not ready or that he was not adequate for the task. Either would have been a sensible way to think about oneself in a huge job like this one. The Lord is able to make Himself known to us just as He is able to help us follow through with the task He gives us. He assured Joshua of who He is and what He was going to do, and Joshua heard Him. May you know Him and hear His voice. If you have not, might you ask Him today?

✦

> "I BECAME A SERVANT OF THE GOSPEL BY THE GIFT OF GOD'S GRACE GIVEN ME BY THE WORKING OF HIS POWER." - EPHESIANS 3:7

**Read Joshua 1; John 10:4b**
What is the dilemma? For Joshua? For the Israelites?

# JOSHUA

DAY TWO - WHAT IS THE DILEMMA?

# JOSHUA

DAY THREE - WHAT IS GOD'S RESCUE?

*The Lord is invested in us, in every detail of our lives*

God cares about all that pertains to His children. Through His lovingkindness and power throughout scripture, God demonstrates who He is and what He does for His people in His name. God cares about His name that the entire earth will know Him. He does not want even one person to die without knowing Him. God could use whomever He chooses to enter the land He had promised to Abraham, Isaac, and Jacob.

God opened Joshua's heart to hear Him and to heed His voice. God's investment in Joshua's life is clear to us as we read God's detailed instructions to Joshua. It is true for each of God's children that God is wholly invested in the details of our lives. His voice through His word and His Holy Spirit are available to us at all times to guide us in the minute and the monumental; God sees us through the lens of Creator, Savior, and Father. He is the Giver of all good things; there is nothing that He withholds from His own. In Christ alone, we have all we need for every detail of our lives.

As God led him into the Promised Land and all that follows on the Israelites' journey to gain possession of it, Joshua leaned into God's instructions. What part of your life needs valuable instruction from the Lord? He is able to provide whatever you may need. Have you asked Him to enter into your life?

Do you know that God wants to be involved in every aspect? Often, we compartmentalize our lives to the parts we want God to be involved in and the components we keep barricaded off. Sometimes, we may not know that we have places we do not want to share with Him; however, God gives all of Himself to us for us to be free in every part of our lives, the places where we feel shame and the places we do not want to go.

Was Joshua's fear an issue God wanted Joshua to face and depend on Him for? God's investment in us is key to our understanding of who He is and who we are to Him. May you know God's investment in you through His Son, Jesus Christ.

---

> "I PRAY OUT OF HIS GLORIOUS RICHES HE MAY STRENGTHEN YOU WITH POWER THROUGH HIS SPIRIT IN YOUR INNER BEING..." - EPHESIANS 3:16

**Read Joshua 3-4**
What is God's rescue? How does God provide?

# JOSHUA

DAY THREE - WHAT IS GOD'S RESCUE?

# JOSHUA

DAY FOUR - WHAT IS THE RESULT OF GOD'S RESCUE?

*The Lord values our rest and He gives us rest because we need it*

God's word gave Joshua what he needed to instruct the spies to search out the land and to defeat Jericho. At each juncture, God's presence was the help Joshua and the Israelites required to be able to move forward on their journey into the Promised Land. It was especially significant as they crossed the Jordan River on dry ground. God knows our limits. His rescue at just the perfect moment drives this point home; as the last person crossed the dry river bed, the water rose again not one second too soon. God values the makeup of each of His children; He knows our frame and that we are but dust. God does not tax us unnecessarily; He gives us rest.

The term, "rest," means several things: to rest physically, emotionally, and spiritually; it also means to trust in God, to depend on Him. In scripture, "rest" sometimes means refreshment for the soul. Another perspective on "rest" in God's word is that God gives us rest while He fights for us. In the defeat of Jericho and the crossing of the Jordan, God gave the instructions and as they obeyed and rested in Him, God fought the enemy for them and gave them the victory. This picture of "rest" is quite different from how we ordinarily think of it in human terms.

God has the whole picture and advocates for us, especially for our rest. What form of "rest" do you need? Have you inquired of God for your rest? He is ready and waiting for you to ask Him. He values you and your propensity for resting in Him in all ways, getting away from the fray, depending on Him, letting Him fight for you, and for refreshment for your soul.

Joshua needed the courage to trust God in all ways; God gave Joshua the means to trust and obey Him which meant to listen and heed the instructions and to take the leadership of the people to move forward under God's leading. The Lord knew what Joshua needed, and He knows what we need too.

✦

> "(YOU) MAY HAVE POWER, TOGETHER WITH ALL THE LORD'S HOLY PEOPLE, TO GRASP HOW WIDE AND LONG AND HIGH AND DEEP IS THE LOVE OF CHRIST AND TO KNOW THAT THIS LOVE SURPASSES KNOWLEDGE THAT YOU MAY BE FILLED TO THE MEASURE OF ALL THE FULLNESS OF GOD" - EPHESIANS 3:18-19

**Read Joshua 2-6; Proverbs 3:5-6**

What is the result of God's rescue? What happens in these passages? What is their response to God's rescue?

# JOSHUA

DAY FOUR - WHAT IS THE RESULT OF GOD'S RESCUE?

# JOSHUA

DAY FIVE - WHAT IS THE "STORY FOR GOD'S GLORY?"

*Day Five: What is "the story for God's glory?"*

In these first chapters of Joshua, we see the Lord showing up and keeping His promises of the generations before them. For Joshua's life, God was real and a very present help. To do what the Lord commanded, he would have to lean on God more for each part of the journey. The Lord works this way in our lives too. The hard things help us depend on God more. We tend to do it on our own when we can, but God knows we need Him even when we don't.

Joshua's life and purpose could not be accomplished without the help of the Lord. God's fulfillment of the Promised Land was no ordinary thing for the people of God, nor was Joshua's leadership of crossing into it. Have you ever been presented a challenge so great that to accomplish it, the Lord would have to be in it lest it would fail? Joshua had this sort of challenge. This is when in our lives God becomes the main character. It is in the difficult, the extraordinary, when depending on the Lord is everything. He is everything. What is your everything? Think about this over the next days. Who is the Lord in your life?

God knows our past, present, and future, the road ahead. Following Him will get us where we should go with Him. To answer the Lord is to say, "Yes."

✦

> "FINALLY, BE STRONG IN THE LORD AND IN HIS MIGHTY POWER."
> - EPHESIANS 6:10

### Read Joshua 24

What is "the story for God's glory?" in Joshua's life and story? How is Joshua's relationship with God different at the end of the story from when he sent out the spies?

# JOSHUA

DAY FIVE - WHAT IS THE "STORY FOR GOD'S GLORY?"

The Power of the Resurrection in Joshua's Life

# JOSHUA

DAY SIX - WHAT ARE GOD'S TRUTHS?

*Trusting God while entering the new land; the new life with Him*

God promised Joshua that He would never leave him nor forsake him as he led the people into the Promised Land. God created Joshua for this moment, for such a time as this. Joshua was the right hand to Moses; so, he knew what he was getting into. However, Moses had not led them into the Promised Land. The one who had been with God and brought the messages from God down to the people did not enter the land, which was given to them. What a daunting task the Lord had saved for him. God also knew the heart of Joshua and that he would need encouragement in the voice of the Lord to him. God promised never to leave him or forsake him, that He would be with Him and would lead the into the land which God had promised. God was faithful, and He would do it.

What has God promised? Never to leave us nor forsake us. Am I living this out? Believing that He is with me and will never leave me? The power of the presence of God is the power of the resurrection. What parts of my life have I not surrendered to God, the one who fulfills His promises like no other? He is a God of promise and the One and Only who fulfills them. Do I believe it? May we take Him at His word that He will never leave or forsake us, that we can be strong and courageous in Him.

✦

> "BUT WHEN HE, THE SPIRIT OF TRUTH, COMES, HE WILL GUIDE YOU INTO ALL THE TRUTH." - JOHN 16:13A

**Reflect on the truths of God from Joshua's life.**
What have you learned about Joshua's relationship with God and who God became to him?
Reflect on God's truths for your own life.

God Fulfills His Promises

# JOSHUA

DAY SIX - WHAT ARE GOD'S TRUTHS?

# A PERSPECTIVE

GOD'S CALL IS TO KNOW HIM AND THE POWER OF THE RESURRECTION

To know Jesus is to know suffering, struggle, difficulty, and pain. The means to become dependent on our Savior and Lord Jesus is to come to the end of ourselves. The power of the resurrection becomes real to us when we do not have the capacity to live as we desire or reach a dream, and we cry out to the One who does, the One who gave us life and the desire to live in hope and truth.

The spacious place is the place where God intervenes, allows, or guides us for the purpose of us knowing Him better. His power to give us Himself is never more profound or necessary than when we cannot remedy or run from the place we have encountered in our lives, albeit a deep and long struggle, an incurable disease, a great loss, a dream deferred, ongoing suffering, or debilitating relational pain. God shows up in grace and power to give us who He is if we will receive the extraordinary gift. As we let go of our own devices and allow His to become our own, His power to live a different way emerges. It is a spacious place—His gift to us of grace in Jesus. After all, He has been pursuing us to give us this grace. If we are really true with ourselves, we yearn for it. And yet, God gives it freely.

The turning around of our plight through sin and sorrow to following Him is the reality of a life in Jesus Christ; each of us as a follower of Jesus has a story which God wrote before the creation. The story is the power of the resurrection of Jesus in our lives. It is uniquely our own and part of His greater one. He delights to give us Himself, a spacious place. Full of grace and opportunity to know Him better, this place offers us comfort, joy, peace, and hope in Him. With every difficult moment, we have the counterpart to it, to know Him in it. We will not find rest without Him or a respite from it without Him in it. He is the spacious place for us.

In Him, we have His power to overcome, to walk through, and to let go of ourselves. This power is the same as the power God used to resurrect Jesus from the dead. We die to how we wish to overcome or walk the journey of life and come alive in the provision of His power and grace to live the story He has given us. It is truly one of His creation and imagination for the world to see Him and who He is. We are a story within a greater one, His. And so here we are, living out His story to proclaim the power of the resurrection of Jesus in a life, yours and mine, just as God wrote about each of our ancestors of the faith in the Bible for us to know Him and the power of the resurrection. From the difficulties of life to the wonder of our Creator, Father, and Lord Jesus Christ is the journey of each child of God—the power of the resurrection for all the world to see and to know Him.

*Walking by Faith*

God steps in to help us walk the walk of faith. The grandeur of our Almighty chooses to live within us. He gives us a place to rest in Him with all that we need to live out the life of abundance He designed for us.

- From our hopelessness to His great hope
- From our sinful and depraved state to His great grace, His unfailing love, and forgiveness
- From our strong-willed and blind position to His Holy Spirit to guide and lead
- From our very weak and frail human condition to His great power within

Our daily walk with Him must be led and guided by Him. Leaning into the faith He bestows upon us by receiving it in full gives us the capacity necessary for the abounding nature He has heaped upon us. Remembering that all that is in this day is grace from above, we know Our great God, who increases our own faithfulness by guiding us back to His grace that He lavishes upon us.

✦

Are you walking by faith? Would you like to walk by faith?

PART X

# DAVID

GOD KNOWS

MORE OF GOD IN OUR LIVES AND STORIES

HAVE MERCY ON ME, MY GOD, HAVE MERCY ON ME, FOR IN YOU I TAKE REFUGE. I WILL TAKE REFUGE IN THE SHADOW OF YOUR WINGS UNTIL THE DISASTER HAS PASSED. I CRY OUT TO GOD MOST HIGH, TO GOD, WHO VINDICATES ME. HE SENDS FROM HEAVEN AND SAVES ME. REBUKING THOSE WHO HOTLY PURSUE ME— GOD SENDS FORTH HIS LOVE AND HIS FAITHFULNESS. I AM IN THE MIDST OF LIONS; I AM FORCED TO DWELL AMONG RAVENOUS BEASTS— MEN WHOSE TEETH ARE SPEARS AND ARROWS, WHOSE TONGUES ARE SHARP SWORDS. BE EXALTED, O GOD, ABOVE THE HEAVENS; LET YOUR GLORY BE OVER ALL THE EARTH. THEY SPREAD A NET FOR MY FEET— I WAS BOWED DOWN IN DISTRESS. THEY DUG A PIT IN MY PATH— BUT THEY HAVE FALLEN INTO IT THEMSELVES. MY HEART, O GOD, IS STEADFAST, MY HEART IS STEADFAST; I WILL SING AND MAKE MUSIC AWAKE, MY SOUL! AWAKE, HARP AND LYRE! I WILL AWAKEN THE DAWN. I WILL PRAISE YOU, LORD, AMONG THE NATIONS; I WILL SING OF YOU AMONG THE PEOPLES. FOR GREAT IS YOUR LOVE, REACHING TO THE HEAVENS; YOUR FAITHFULNESS REACHES TO THE SKIES. BE EXALTED, O GOD, ABOVE THE HEAVENS; LET YOUR GLORY BE OVER ALL THE EARTH.

PSALM 57

PART X

# DAVID

GOD KNOWS

Samuel anointed David to be king years before David actually became the King of Israel. Not only did his brothers or father not think that he would be the one God chose, Samuel also did not see it. Yet, God chooses whom He chooses for His purposes. It was David's lineage that was chosen for the long-awaited Messiah; Jesus would come from the descendants of David. God also called David, a man after God's own heart.

God saw David's heart. He told Samuel not to look at the physical appearance of the one to be anointed king, but that it was the heart of the king God wanted. It's the same for us; God is interested in our hearts. One doesn't have to study David's life very long to see how God gave him a heart for God with the ability to worship and confess his sin and the capacity to know the heart of God.

God wants us to have hearts that are moldable into ones that receive and rely upon His love for us. We cannot love God without His first loving us; we also cannot love Him in return without His giving us the ability to love Him. David knew the rescue of God in his life.

✦

**Mystery**
By God, one may be described as "a man after God's own heart."

**Power**
The power and love of God are demonstrated in that Jesus died for us while we were still sinners.

**Paradox**
Not only does God want our hearts, He also gives us hearts that want Him.

The Power of the Resurrection in David's Life

# DAVID

DAY ONE - WHO IS GOD?

*God knows His plans for us, one for a hope and a future*

God knows the deep and long held hurts of our past. He knows the fears and anxiety we have about our present and our future. He surely knows how we have coped and how we are going to choose to cope in the future. God knew the heart of David and knows each of ours too. He loves us despite our ways and runs after us to rescue us from ourselves. David hid; he ran; he outsmarted King Saul, who wanted to kill him. David also ran from his own family responsibilities and from those of a king at war. God allowed the hard journey, and God knew that David would turn around back to Him as His Father God, the desire of his heart. Out of God's lovingkindness, He gave David the capacity in his brokenness to bring him back to the plans God had for him, plans for a future and hope in God.

Do you know that God has plans for you, plans for a future and a hope? Are you running, hiding, or sabotaging your life with plans of your own? Our plans are just that—ours. God's purpose and plans for our lives are so much greater and encompass so much more. His imagination and rescue have built in them the best for us, which always demonstrate who the Lord of Glory is, the One and Only Lord, Jesus Christ.

Are you willing to surrender your plans to His?

✦

> "I PRAY THAT THE EYES OF YOUR HEART MAY BE ENLIGHTENED IN ORDER THAT YOU MAY KNOW THE HOPE TO WHICH HE HAS CALLED YOU, THE RICHES OF HIS GLORIOUS INHERITANCE IN HIS HOLY PEOPLE, AND HIS INCOMPARABLY GREAT POWER FOR US WHO BELIEVE. THAT POWER IS THE SAME AS THE MIGHTY STRENGTH HE EXERTED WHEN HE RAISED CHRIST FROM THE DEAD AND SEATED HIM AT HIS RIGHT HAND IN THE HEAVENLY REALMS ..." - EPHESIANS 1:18-20

**Read 1 Samuel 16; Jeremiah 29:11**
Who is God? Who is He in these scripture passages?

# DAVID

DAY ONE - WHO IS GOD?

# DAVID

DAY TWO - WHAT IS THE DILEMMA?

*God knows the hearts of His children and loves us so*

God loves us in our circumstances. He comes with lovingkindness and might. It is required in order to pry us free from the entrapment we find ourselves in. Only God can and will free us to follow His path. The enemies of Israel taunted them with their strength, physicality, and numbers; yet, God remained with the Israelites. David, the young shepherd, knew His Lord and could not stand the jabs and terrible lies about the Lord their God. With the Almighty God as His advocate, wisdom, and strength, David aimed his weapon at Goliath. God defeated the enemy. He comes to our rescue because He loves us so much. God Almighty fought the enemy, and in their defeat, they knew it was the Lord. As God shows forth His might and His love, the world knows it is He.

God uses David's accounts of his life through the scripture in the Psalms to show us who He is and what He has done. David's heartfelt cries for mercy, provision, and for dealing with his enemies led him into praises of the Good Lord he knew so well. Amidst his terrible relationships with Saul, his own children, and others in his life, David turns to the Lord for help. God shows us His heart for his children through the prayers and praises of David.

Do you know that the Lord fights for you? He has already won the battle through the death and resurrection of His Only Son, Jesus. He has done it once and for all. As He pursues us out of His love for us, He continues to fight for us. Amidst all of our running away, turning away, and running from Him in shame, God still loves us.

---

> "I BECAME A SERVANT OF THE GOSPEL BY THE GIFT OF GOD'S GRACE GIVEN ME BY THE WORKING OF HIS POWER." - EPHESIANS 3:7

**Read 1 Samuel 17; Psalm 25**
What is the dilemma? What problem does David face?

# DAVID

DAY TWO - WHAT IS THE DILEMMA?

The Power of the Resurrection in David's Life

# DAVID

DAY THREE - WHAT IS GOD'S RESCUE?

*God knows the paths we will choose and loves us still*

God has a plan for each of us. He created a purpose for His children before we were born. We are His handiwork, His own. David, the youngest of Jesse's sons, was out in the pasture with the sheep when Samuel, the prophet, came to anoint a new king. God's anointing was based on the heart and not on the outward appearance. He anointed David king when he was fifteen years old, and David would wait fifteen years to take the reign. God anoints each of His children with a plan and a purpose based on a heart to follow Him. He establishes our hearts to be able to know and follow Him.

Our hearts given by God demonstrate the inner workings of our beings. God knows our hearts and the steps we will take. To follow God with our lives, we must surrender our hearts to Him. David, the shepherd boy anointed king, knew the heart of God. It says in Psalm 78 that David had "integrity of heart." David knew the single-mindedness of loving the Lord God with all of his heart, soul, mind, and strength. Even though he did not always follow God's heart, God also gave him the capacity to repent and to return. David's choices did not always reflect the heart of a child of God, and neither do ours. But God in the riches of His great grace gives us the capacity to know what pleases Him and what does not and also the capacity to be humble and turn away from the things which we choose that are not pleasing to Him.

Do you know the plans God has for you? Are your plans lining up with the ones the Lord has chosen for you? Is there a path which you are choosing that is not pleasing to the Lord?

✦

> "I PRAY OUT OF HIS GLORIOUS RICHES HE MAY STRENGTHEN YOU WITH POWER THROUGH HIS SPIRIT IN YOUR INNER BEING…" - EPHESIANS 3:16

**Read 2 Samuel 11; Psalm 32**
What is God's rescue? How does God provide for David? For us?

# DAVID

DAY THREE - WHAT IS GOD'S RESCUE?

# DAVID

DAY FOUR - WHAT IS THE RESULT OF GOD'S RESCUE?

*God listens to the hearts of His own and guides and leads them in His ways*

God gave David a fresh start; he does the same with us. In scripture it says that David had "integrity of heart." Integrity means single-mindedness of honor. God gives us this capacity. We do not have it of our own volition. David's many passions led him astray, including the affair with Bathsheba. But with God's heart, David was able to repent, turn around, ask for God's forgiveness, and move forward in worship of God. The broken and repentant heart are evident in many of David's psalms.

With each transgression or stepping away from God, we have the opportunity to turn back in humility and ask for God's mercy. We do not deserve God's lovingkindness, but He has given it in full in Jesus Christ. David grieved his affair and actions with Bathsheba. Psalm 51 details his conversation with our Living Lord petitioning His forgiveness and grace for a new heart. God honors us with His extension of grace through Jesus Christ while we were sinners. This grace is available to us each day as we follow Him when we misstep. He gives us a fresh start, a clean slate, and a new heart to worship and follow Him.

God is waiting for us to choose and rely on Him to guide and lead us in His ways rather than our own. When we turn toward Him, we receive not only new hearts but more of God Himself. How are you doing choosing God's ways instead of your own?

---

> "(YOU) MAY HAVE POWER, TOGETHER WITH ALL THE LORD'S HOLY PEOPLE, TO GRASP HOW WIDE AND LONG AND HIGH AND DEEP IS THE LOVE OF CHRIST AND TO KNOW THAT THIS LOVE SURPASSES KNOWLEDGE THAT YOU MAY BE FILLED TO THE MEASURE OF ALL THE FULLNESS OF GOD" - EPHESIANS 3:18-19

**Read Psalm 51**
What is the result of God's rescue? How does David respond to God's rescue?

# DAVID

DAY FOUR - WHAT IS THE RESULT OF GOD'S RESCUE?

# DAVID

DAY FIVE - WHAT IS THE "STORY FOR GOD'S GLORY?"

*No matter how wayward God's child is, God knows what He accomplishes in His zeal in the life of His child with the redemption through Jesus Christ*

God sent Nathan to confront David with his sin. The scripture includes David's response to the prophet, Nathan, and how he reacts to the sin in the story Nathan tells him. Confronted by his own sin, David grieves and mourns his actions and his loss. Are we truly repentant for the ways we have wronged others and sinned against God? Has the Lord confronted our sin?

Jesus came to confront as well as to extend grace and mercy. We who receive the confrontation and recognize that we are the sinners will be given mercy from the One and Only Jesus Christ when we choose to turn away from our waywardness and come home to God.

David knew the sin in his heart and confessed it to the Lord; he also did not expect the consequences of his actions to disappear. The Lord was gracious in his forgiveness and also merciful with His justice. Do we ever want justice for ourselves, or is it that we always want justice for someone else who has wronged us? Jesus does not show favoritism. We all sin and fall short; He comes to save each one of us from our depravity. He died so that we may all have eternal life with Him. God showed David how much he needed the lovingkindness of the Savior, Jesus Christ.

✦

> "FINALLY, BE STRONG IN THE LORD AND IN HIS MIGHTY POWER."
> - EPHESIANS 6:10

**Read 2 Samuel 12; Psalm 78**
What is "the story for God's glory?" How has God provided for David through failure?
And for you through failure?

# DAVID

DAY FIVE - WHAT IS THE "STORY FOR GOD'S GLORY?"

# DAVID

DAY SIX - WHAT ARE GOD'S TRUTHS?

*Trusting God with our whole heart*

God knows all. He knew David's heart. He gave David the ability to know God's heart for him too. David knew God loved him and cared for him by protecting him and giving him means of escape from his nemesis, Saul. David worshipped the Lord and knew how to sing praises and also how to repent to God of his errant ways. David knew the grace and compassion of the Lord.

When David sinned with Bathsheba, it led him to do many more terrible things like putting her husband on the front lines so that he would be killed. David knew his selfish and sinful ways and yet had to be reminded of them. Nathan, the prophet, told David a story about the man who used another's innocent lamb as a sacrifice, and David was incensed. Nathan remarked that it was what David had done. David knew his sin, and he went to God in prayer and repentance. We see his remorse and broken and contrite heart in Psalm 51. God knew all of David's heart, the good, the bad, and the ugly; yet, He forgave him. He forgives us of our sin when we come to Him.

God knows my heart. He also knows that He has saved me from myself. What else does He know? May I live with Him and talk to Him about everything. And repent and turn around as God showed David how to do (in the Psalms) and also, at the same time, receive His grace. When we wander off from God, He waits for us to return. But He also allows the consequences of our behavior. David knew the consequences and accepted them and returned to the Lord. Where are we to go when we have wandered off but back to Him? God takes our broken places, and in addition to mending them, He gives us more of Himself. May we return with our sorrowful hearts to receive more of God's heart. This is who He is. God gave David the capacity to know Him. May we know Him more and more.

✦

> "BUT WHEN HE, THE SPIRIT OF TRUTH, COMES, HE WILL GUIDE YOU INTO ALL THE TRUTH." - JOHN 16:13A

**Reflect on the truths of God you have learned from David's life.**
What have you learned about God from David's life and story? How is God different from what you may have expected and known before this study of God's word in David's life?

# DAVID

DAY SIX - WHAT ARE GOD'S TRUTHS?

The Power of the Resurrection in David's Life

# A PERSPECTIVE

## GOD'S PLAN FOR US—RECEIVING ALL IN JESUS CHRIST

God gives us the capacity in the Holy Spirit to receive what He has already given in Jesus Christ. First, He gives us the ability to repent of our sin and to acknowledge that He is Lord and Savior in our lives. Then He equips us daily to follow Him:

- To confess our sin and to turn toward Him as our God and Savior in Jesus Christ
- To live with joy and peace, regardless of our circumstances
- To leave, go, lead, rule, teach, be bold, see, and to see God
- To let go of something one holds tightly
- To have strength
- To have wisdom
- To have humility and be humble
- To be holy as He is holy
- To persevere through the difficult: illness, loss, betrayal, disappointment
- To pray with humility, faith, and persistence
- To believe, trust God, and lean into Him
- To study His word and gain insight into who God is and what He says and what He does
- To allow God to work within
- To obey God and follow Him
- To be available for God to teach and to guide
- To allow God to fill our empty places with Himself

All that He has, He has given to us in Jesus Christ. It is done already. What if we were to receive the grace extended to us this day for such a time as this? He imagines "life to the full" for each of us. May we live each day according to God's imagination, by His plan for us, and His desire for us to have the measure of all the fullness of God, which He says is within our reach because He has already given it, more than we ask or imagine. Yet, it is not beyond our Lord's imagination. He wants us to have MORE of Him, the MORE we can never get to the end of, the MORE that is Jesus.

✦

Have you given your life to Jesus Christ? Do you know Him as your Lord and Savior?

PART XI

# ANNA

GOD PROVIDES

MORE OF GOD IN OUR LIVES AND STORIES

THERE WAS ALSO A PROPHET, ANNA, THE DAUGHTER OF PENUEL, OF THE TRIBE OF ASHER. SHE WAS VERY OLD; SHE HAD LIVED WITH HER HUSBAND SEVEN YEARS AFTER HER MARRIAGE, AND THEN WAS A WIDOW UNTIL SHE WAS EIGHTY-FOUR. SHE NEVER LEFT THE TEMPLE BUT WORSHIPED NIGHT AND DAY, FASTING AND PRAYING. COMING UP TO THEM AT THAT VERY MOMENT, SHE GAVE THANKS TO GOD AND SPOKE ABOUT THE CHILD TO ALL WHO WERE LOOKING FORWARD TO THE REDEMPTION OF JERUSALEM.

LUKE 1:36-38

# PART XI
# ANNA
## GOD PROVIDES

There is little scripture about Anna; yet, the few verses demonstrate the power and purpose of God in a life of one who believes in Him. Anna lived a life of prayer, and God honored her with a life of great purpose.

Do we know our purpose in the one life God gives us, a rich and full one in Christ Jesus? Anna did, and she spent her years in the temple of her Lord. God gave her the ability to see after all the years of praying and fasting in the temple. Her dream of seeing the Messiah fulfilled by the Lord became reality for her when Jesus came into the temple.

✦

**Mystery**
God creates in us the unique abilities only He gives, and with them, He has given us purpose for His kingdom.

**Power**
The power of the resurrection became real to Anna when Jesus came to the temple. Only with the sight the Lord gave her could she see the real Messiah in Jesus as He entered the temple.

**Paradox**
Anna knew her purpose even if the people and the community did not. Her purpose from God also gave her capacity to see the answer to her prayers.

The Power of the Resurrection in Anna's Life

# ANNA

DAY ONE - WHO IS GOD?

*God guides us into His purpose*

God determined His purpose for each of our lives before creation. As we follow Him, He creates the means in which to accomplish the purpose He has set forth in us. In Philippians 1:6, it says, "He who began a good work in us will be faithful to complete until the day of Christ Jesus."

Anna knew the Lord and practiced her faith to her faithful God. When her husband died after only a short seven years, Anna was widowed and alone. She would not have a source of provision, except through the temple. Anna prayed night and day in the temple, and the Lord provided for her as she gave her days to Him. God's purpose for her unfolded as she gave her life to His cause, the redemption through Jesus Christ.

When Mary and Joseph brought Jesus into the temple, Anna's heartfelt dreams were met. She had seen the Messiah. She knew it was He because she knew the Lord to whom she had been praying and conversing all this time. Do you know Him? How do you know your purpose for this day, for such a time as this?

✦

> "I PRAY THAT THE EYES OF YOUR HEART MAY BE ENLIGHTENED IN ORDER THAT YOU MAY KNOW THE HOPE TO WHICH HE HAS CALLED YOU, THE RICHES OF HIS GLORIOUS INHERITANCE IN HIS HOLY PEOPLE, AND HIS INCOMPARABLY GREAT POWER FOR US WHO BELIEVE. THAT POWER IS THE SAME AS THE MIGHTY STRENGTH HE EXERTED WHEN HE RAISED CHRIST FROM THE DEAD AND SEATED HIM AT HIS RIGHT HAND IN THE HEAVENLY REALMS ..." - EPHESIANS 1:18-20

**Read Luke 2; Ephesians 2:10; Deuteronomy 33:24-29**
*Note: Anna was a descendant of the tribe of Asher, one of the twelve tribes of Israel*
Who is God in these scripture passages?

# ANNA

DAY ONE - WHO IS GOD?

The Power of the Resurrection in Anna's Life

# ANNA

DAY TWO - WHAT IS THE DILEMMA?

*God knows the hopes and desires of our hearts*

Anna prayed that her hopes and desires for the Messiah would become reality and that she would see Him. Her focus was resolute; God gave her a special dream and prayer. The end result of her life work after her husband died was the redemption of all mankind through the Messiah, Jesus Christ. How is it that she knew to pray and to spend her time on her knees to this end? I believe that God placed this on her heart. He uses His children to bring about His purposes. As a child of God, we have the opportunity to collaborate and join with Him in His mission for all the world.

Anna took part in the greater story as she knew the main character in her own. This is how God works in a life of a child of His; He loves each one so much that He would give His Only Son to have a relationship with him. Anna's heart and life changed forever with the Messiah's coming as have each of ours. May you know and see the Savior today. She prayed the desire of her heart. Would you consider talking to God about the deep and heartfelt ache within you, a hope or a dream perhaps, that has not become a reality? Anna did, and imagine her joy on the day Jesus came to the temple.

✦

> "I BECAME A SERVANT OF THE GOSPEL BY THE GIFT OF GOD'S GRACE GIVEN ME BY THE WORKING OF HIS POWER." - EPHESIANS 3:7

**Read Psalm 37:4**
What is the dilemma for Anna?

# ANNA

DAY TWO - WHAT IS THE DILEMMA?

# ANNA

DAY THREE - WHAT IS GOD'S RESCUE?

*God doesn't leave us in our troubles, and His presence gives us rest*

Anna was a widow in a day when men held the economic reigns and inheritance; she was left without means to live. Yet, God was her provider and her sustainer. She made it clear to all that she was solely dependent on Him. God did not leave her alone; He was present with her daily. As she left her needs and desires at the altar daily, God provided.

Her rest in her loving Lord was a symbol to all who entered. She prayed and rested in the Lord's sovereignty in her life. What are we not at rest about? Is God not in control of all? Where do we place our trust? Are we able to rest without control?

Anna likely had many reservations about life after her husband's death. She was human and a woman in her day; everyone knew the plight. But Anna did not give up. She asked the Lord. She petitioned the Lord. She rested in the Lord day and night. His presence was real to her.

May we see Him as she did. Do you think that her faith became sight because of her prayers?

✦

> "I PRAY OUT OF HIS GLORIOUS RICHES HE MAY STRENGTHEN YOU WITH POWER THROUGH HIS SPIRIT IN YOUR INNER BEING..." - EPHESIANS 3:16

**Read Psalm 34**
What is God's rescue for Anna? How does He provide and care for her?

# ANNA

DAY THREE - WHAT IS GOD'S RESCUE?

# ANNA

DAY FOUR - WHAT IS THE RESULT OF GOD'S RESCUE?

*God's provision is for our good and His glory*

God does not withhold any good thing from His children. Anna's life did not look so good to an outsider. Sometimes our lives do not look so good or feel so good. Our view of circumstances sometimes limits our perspective. God says that He rescues and He provides. Do we believe Him?

What is your perspective on your life circumstances at the moment? Is there great stress or struggle in your family or work? What do you see lacking? Your great need is the vehicle for God's great grace. Anna's life story reflects this about our Great God. He answers us in our great need of Him. He knows our need and becomes real to us through it.

As He answers our great need for Him, He shows us who he is and what He does for His children, His glory for all the world to see. Might your great need today be the invitation from God Himself to enter in to His great grace.

✦

> "(YOU) MAY HAVE POWER, TOGETHER WITH ALL THE LORD'S HOLY PEOPLE, TO GRASP HOW WIDE AND LONG AND HIGH AND DEEP IS THE LOVE OF CHRIST AND TO KNOW THAT THIS LOVE SURPASSES KNOWLEDGE THAT YOU MAY BE FILLED TO THE MEASURE OF ALL THE FULLNESS OF GOD" - EPHESIANS 3:18-19

**Read Psalm 91**
What is the result of God's rescue of Anna? Of us? How does the psalmist respond?

# ANNA

DAY FOUR - WHAT IS THE RESULT OF GOD'S RESCUE?

The Power of the Resurrection in Anna's Life

# ANNA

DAY FIVE - WHAT IS THE "STORY FOR GOD'S GLORY?"

*God's provision is more than we ask or imagine*

What are you seeking today that is beyond your reach? God knows. How have you handled it thus far? Have you asked Him about it? Anna sought the Lord about seeing the Messiah in her day. She cried out to Him daily for it. Have you been praying and seeking the Lord for a long time? God hears before we call on Him.

Sometimes we wait, seemingly on God. But I believe perhaps the reality is that God is waiting for us. Might He be building in us the growth and perspective to receive His great grace? Could it be that He has something much better than what we are seeking?

God's provision for us is more of Himself. At our deepest core, God is the only one who will fill our every want and desire. And when we recognize this truth, we know the Living Lord and how much He loves us as He shows us who He is through the relationship with Him. Anna knew her hope and dreams were in Him because He placed them within her. His answer was more than she imagined.

May we see and know Him more and more. It is greater than we ask or imagine.

✦

> "FINALLY, BE STRONG IN THE LORD AND IN HIS MIGHTY POWER." - EPHESIANS 6:10

**Read Psalm 103**
What is "the story for God's glory?" Why do you think Anna saw the Lord in the temple?

# ANNA

DAY FIVE - WHAT IS THE "STORY FOR GOD'S GLORY?"

The Power of the Resurrection in Anna's Life

# ANNA

DAY SIX - WHAT ARE GOD'S TRUTHS?

*Trusting God with all of our lives, every detail*

God provided for Anna her entire life. He knew her dreams and her prayers before she prayed them. God knew that Anna would be widowed at an early age. He had a plan for her life which included her ministry of prayer and fasting. God gave her a heart for the life He bestowed upon her. Anna petitioned the Lord for her every need and for the dream she had of seeing her Messiah.

God allowed Anna to know Him as the provider of her soul, her life, and her all. She got it: He was her all. She knew the Lord, and we can too. Do you know Him as the provider of your life purpose? Do you know that He also handles every need down to the smallest detail of your life?

In addition to the great purpose God provides for each of our lives, God provides the smallest of things. He knows ours need before we ask Him. What am I lacking that I have not asked God about? Do I know what God has in store for me as His purpose in my life?

May we give Him the entire landscape of our lives, and in turn, may we come to know the Lord as the provider of all. He makes our lives into ones of purpose, and He provides the details to make it so.

✦

> "BUT WHEN HE, THE SPIRIT OF TRUTH, COMES, HE WILL GUIDE YOU INTO ALL THE TRUTH."
> - JOHN 16:13A

**Reflect on the truths of God which you have learned from Anna's life.**
How does God show up for Anna? For each of us?
What truth of God did you learn from her life and story? And your own?

# ANNA

DAY SIX - WHAT ARE GOD'S TRUTHS?

# A PERSPECTIVE
GOD IS ALWAYS WITH US AND IS SOVEREIGN OVER ALL

God has already chosen His own. He does not want one of His children to live without Him. Yet, He requires that we choose Him back. He pursues us and waits, but He tells us that we must seek Him while He may be found. (Isaiah 55:6)

A vignette for illustration, "Get in the car:" When our son was a middle schooler, he did not want to go with the program at times. He wasn't sure what he wanted or it seemed that way to me, but he thought he didn't want our way. So many times, I would say, "Get in the car." I meant business that he just needed to obey me (us). He would do it, and things would go more smoothly. He needed direction, and I believe that within himself, he knew this and also felt better with the boundaries we had set for him as a child in our home. God knows us; He created us; He knows what is best for us. However, our Lord is not one to push or control us to follow Him. We must decide to trust and obey. When we do, we realize that He has been waiting on us and pursuing us for the ride with Him.

When we do, the Lord sometimes carries us. God delights in rescuing us (Psalm 18:19), and He is distressed when we are distressed (Isaiah 63:9).

Sometimes, we have to climb mountains. We must persevere, and He helps us (James 1:2-3).

God is silent it sometimes seems to us. He is God; there is no other (1Kings 8:60).

And sometimes, we must wait. No eye has seen, nor ear has heard, nor mind conceived the things God has prepared for those who love Him (1 Cor 2:9) and (Isaiah 64:4).

In all, we may have what He has freely given us in Jesus, and that is rest for our souls. "Come to me, all you who are weary and burdened, and I will give you rest. Take my yoke upon you and learn from me, for I am gentle and humble in heart, and you will find rest for your souls. For my yoke is easy and my burden is light" (Matthew 11:28-30).

During the dilemma when we want to move on, out, and most of the time, we want to avoid moving through, several things occur. We have to decide who is in the lead, the driver seat, the center of our lives. Do we need help and to whom are we going to direct our cries for help? It is easy to try to manage it ourselves in the same ways we have managed other parts of our lives. Perhaps this time it does not work. We are at the end of ourselves. What do we do?

If we determine we are going to cry out to God, He already knows and is ready for us. However, we may not go this way even though God is pursuing us through the dilemma. He is there for the rescue, the climb, the wait, and the silence. He is loving us through whether we know it or not. If we cry out to Him, it does not guarantee an easier path. God comes with us to hold us, walk with us, to give us courage to climb or painstakingly step through, and to wait, even wait in the silence.

I am still learning to get in the car, to let God drive, and to allow this dilemma to have its place in my life. God uses all things to His glory and for our good, but we do not experience or know this until we allow Him to lead during one of the hard things we go through in life. I can actually rest when He is in the driver seat; I breathe with assurance He has the problem in hand and will help me through it. His expertise is most necessary; He is God, and there is no other. I am not capable, nor am I reasonably experienced to handle many situations, but He is. I am able by His Holy Spirit to believe Him and to believe He has it and will cover, guide, and protect me through this hard stuff. I can go nowhere He is not; neither will He leave me in it or leave me to my own devices.

Therein lies the crux of the dilemma. I am God's child. He is my Father and desires that I know Him. Through this difficulty, He provides as only He can. He shows us who He is and what He does. He knows our every frailty, and He is aware of the circumstances in which I find myself, even if I had a hand in my own mess, and yet, He loves me still. He knew before I was born that I would have these problems, and He knew exactly how He would help me and love me through them. If I allow Him in the driver seat, He will reveal Himself to me in ways I have not asked or imagined.

Will it be total bliss as He leads us through? Probably not. However, He gives us a glimpse and sometimes more of what He has in mind for us through the struggles, pain, and adversity in our lives. These things He has in mind for us are truth, grace, joy, peace, comfort, and hope. His gifts during the hard things are life-giving. He takes the wounded, broken, and totally shattered pieces of us and turns them into new life. In the places we need Him, He comes and gives us Himself; it is new, and it is the life He imagined for you and for me.

Do I want to suffer? I can say I absolutely do not. But I do know that I have met God in the midst of suffering, and I wouldn't trade it for anything. He is more. I want more of Him.

✦

What might the Lord want you to let go of?

How will you allow the Lord into more of your life?

Write a short prayer of praise and thanksgiving to the Lord for what He has shown you:

PART XII

# LYDIA

GOD GIVES

MORE OF GOD IN OUR LIVES AND STORIES

FROM TROAS WE PUT OUT TO SEA AND SAILED STRAIGHT FOR SAMOTHRACE, AND THE NEXT DAY WE WENT ON TO NEAPOLIS. FROM THERE WE TRAVELED TO PHILIPPI, A ROMAN COLONY AND THE LEADING CITY OF THAT DISTRICT OF MACEDONIA. AND WE STAYED THERE SEVERAL DAYS. ON THE SABBATH WE WENT OUTSIDE THE CITY GATE TO THE RIVER, WHERE WE EXPECTED TO FIND A PLACE OF PRAYER. WE SAT DOWN AND BEGAN TO SPEAK TO THE WOMEN WHO HAD GATHERED THERE. ONE OF THOSE LISTENING WAS A WOMAN FROM THE CITY OF THYATIRA NAMED LYDIA, A DEALER IN PURPLE CLOTH. SHE WAS A WORSHIPER OF GOD. THE LORD OPENED HER HEART TO RESPOND TO PAUL'S MESSAGE. WHEN SHE AND THE MEMBERS OF HER HOUSEHOLD WERE BAPTIZED, SHE INVITED US TO HER HOME. "IF YOU CONSIDER ME A BELIEVER IN THE LORD," SHE SAID, "COME AND STAY AT MY HOUSE." AND SHE PERSUADED US.

ACTS 16:11-15

PART XII

# LYDIA

GOD GIVES

Lydia was one of Paul's first converts. As Paul and his cohorts were looking for a place to pray, they found a group of women gathered on the hillside. Lydia was among them. She became a believer as she listened to Paul share the gospel. Only God! He knew that her heart was ready to receive all of Him. As she did, her entire household also became believers in the living Lord.

Lydia's home became the place where Paul and his companions returned over and over. Her house became a place of worship and a place where people came to know the Lord. God showed up in her life so that she would know Him. And when He did, others came to know the Lord also.

The purpose the Lord gave Lydia was one He had in mind when He made her. What purpose did the Lord have in mind when He created you? Have you asked Him?

✦

### Mystery
The Lord alone knows our hearts and when we are ready to receive Him.

### Power
God's power, evident in Paul's life, became the power that
propelled Lydia into service for her Lord.

### Paradox
God orchestrates all of our moments.

# LYDIA

DAY ONE - WHO IS GOD?

*God knows the extent of our faith*

On the sabbath afternoon the women were gathered by the river. Paul and his companions sat down and began to speak to them. Lydia, a wealthy business woman, listened intently; she was already a worshipper of God. God opened her heart for more, and she and her household were saved on that day. God knew the faith of Lydia's heart and that she needed more of Him in her life.

We do not have to be anything more; God knows exactly where we are. He knows the faith we have, the lack of it, and at any given point, the extreme need we have for Him in our lives. We sometimes think we can fool God or cover our tracks. Often, we don't even consider where we are in our faith lives because we are immersed in the world and ourselves. Lydia's heart was known to God as are ours. God loves and knows everything about us.

What do you want to know about God? May you ask Him?

✦

> "I PRAY THAT THE EYES OF YOUR HEART MAY BE ENLIGHTENED IN ORDER THAT YOU MAY KNOW THE HOPE TO WHICH HE HAS CALLED YOU, THE RICHES OF HIS GLORIOUS INHERITANCE IN HIS HOLY PEOPLE, AND HIS INCOMPARABLY GREAT POWER FOR US WHO BELIEVE. THAT POWER IS THE SAME AS THE MIGHTY STRENGTH HE EXERTED WHEN HE RAISED CHRIST FROM THE DEAD AND SEATED HIM AT HIS RIGHT HAND IN THE HEAVENLY REALMS ..." - EPHESIANS 1:18-20

**Read Acts 16:1-15**
Who is God? Who is He in this scripture passage?

# LYDIA

DAY ONE - WHO IS GOD?

# LYDIA

DAY TWO - WHAT IS THE DILEMMA?

*God pursues us to grow us up in faith*

It is God's pursuit of us that brings about the mystery of our following Him. He loves us with an everlasting love and commitment to us; He wants to spend eternity with each of His own. God pursued Lydia on this Sabbath afternoon by the river because He knew she needed Him to enlarge her faith and her knowledge of Him. God goes to great lengths to love us and draw us closer to Himself.

Have you known this pursuit of God? Are you paying attention to where He has shown up in your life? Is this a new way of thinking about Him? God is waking you up to His presence. Imagine the great God of the universe running after each of us to show us who He is and how much He loves us. Would you stop and listen to His voice as He calls after you? Lydia did; it was the great moment of her life. It could be yours too.

✦

> "I BECAME A SERVANT OF THE GOSPEL BY THE GIFT OF GOD'S GRACE GIVEN ME BY THE WORKING OF HIS POWER." - EPHESIANS 3:7

**Read Hebrews 11**
What is the dilemma? Why are the persons named in Hebrews 11? Why would we read this passage while studying Lydia?

# LYDIA

DAY TWO - WHAT IS THE DILEMMA?

# LYDIA

DAY THREE - WHAT IS GOD'S RESCUE?

*God's mysterious ways are His gifts to us*

There are so many things about God that are mystery to us. We can know Him intimately as He gives us the faith to do so; however, we will never get to the end of God, His love, His commitment to us. It is unfathomable; yet, His ways are gifts. Paul and his companions stopped by the river on that day to talk to the women of which Lydia was one. Only God could orchestrate it. His ways are not ours; only God knows the hearts and acts to save each one of us.

Lydia and her entire family were saved that day. Paul and his crew were in search of a place to pray and started sharing the gospel with the women. Their search became the salvation of souls which was the larger mission of God on this day and this hour. What is God doing in your life right now at this moment? We cannot know the extent of His delight to rescue us, but we surely know Him more and more as we answer His pursuit in Jesus Christ as Lydia did on that day.

Lydia's life changed in a moment. May you answer His call today.

✦

> "I PRAY OUT OF HIS GLORIOUS RICHES HE MAY STRENGTHEN YOU WITH POWER THROUGH HIS SPIRIT IN YOUR INNER BEING…" -EPHESIANS 3:16

**Read 1 Corinthian 2**
What is God's rescue? How does God provide for us? For Lydia? For you?

# LYDIA

DAY THREE - WHAT IS GOD'S RESCUE?

The Power of the Resurrection in Lydia's Life

# LYDIA

DAY FOUR - WHAT IS THE RESULT OF GOD'S RESCUE?

*God knows the ways of our hearts and where we are at all times*

The ways of our hearts are not pure; yet, God loves us anyway. He knows our great need for Him. Lydia found her great need for Him on the day by the river. God opens our hearts to know our need for Him. He knows when we are at a new crossroads in our worship of Him just as He did in Lydia's life. She knew that God was to be worshipped but she did not know Him.

God waits patiently for His own to draw near as He draws near to them. Sometimes it takes a crisis or an intervention. God intervened for Lydia by having Paul address the women and share the good news of Jesus Christ. Do you know the good news of Jesus Christ? Perhaps you know it but have not responded to Him yet? If you have not responded, you have rejected Him. If you are waiting for something to nudge you on, you are also saying no to Him. While we are sinners, He comes to us. We will not be a better version of ourselves at another time. He loves you now and there is nothing you can do or not do to make Him love you any less. Lydia responded to the Living Lord on that day by the river with a resounding "Yes." May you also.

♦

> "(YOU) MAY HAVE POWER, TOGETHER WITH ALL THE LORD'S HOLY PEOPLE, TO GRASP HOW WIDE AND LONG AND HIGH AND DEEP IS THE LOVE OF CHRIST AND TO KNOW THAT THIS LOVE SURPASSES KNOWLEDGE THAT YOU MAY BE FILLED TO THE MEASURE OF ALL THE FULLNESS OF GOD" - EPHESIANS 3:18-19

**Read James 1**
What is the result of God's rescue? What happens as a response to God's rescue?

# LYDIA

DAY FOUR - WHAT IS THE RESULT OF GOD'S RESCUE?

The Power of the Resurrection in Lydia's Life

# LYDIA

DAY FIVE - WHAT IS THE "STORY FOR GOD'S GLORY?"

*God is working in all interactions to bring about His purposes for His glory for all to know Him*

God's working through all for each child's good is not something to be grasped, but we can trust Him in it. Lydia's story gives us a glimpse. She did not pursue Paul and his teaching. Paul did not know Lydia's heart. God does. His love and intention toward each of His own is to give them life and life to the full in Jesus Christ. As He makes Himself known to the one, He demonstrates His love to the world. God's purposes are not our own.

As we read Lydia's story, we find in scripture that this day became the first of many where her home was used for the purposes of the gospel. Paul and his companions came to her after their escape from prison; they gathered, thanked, and praised the Lord. Lydia's life became a vessel used by God for His work and His glory. Is your life being used by God for His work and purpose? Do you want to live for His purposes and to bring glory to Him?

✦

> "FINALLY, BE STRONG IN THE LORD AND IN HIS MIGHTY POWER." - EPHESIANS 6:10

**Read Acts 16:16-40; Hebrews 12**
What is "the story for God's glory?" How does Lydia's story give you hope?

# LYDIA

DAY FIVE - WHAT IS THE "STORY FOR GOD'S GLORY?"

The Power of the Resurrection in Lydia's Life

# LYDIA

DAY SIX - WHAT ARE GOD'S TRUTHS?

*Trusting God with our purpose in life*

God gave Lydia's life purpose. She and her family were saved on the Sabbath as Paul and his crew were trying to find a place to pray and came upon the women meeting on the hillside. Lydia became a host home for the fellowship of believers in their day.

God knew the heart of Lydia, and He wanted her to know His for her. As Paul spoke the truth of the gospel, she and her family were saved on that day. With the salvation of the Savior, God turns our lives into ones of purpose and fulfillment in Him. He has the master plan, and He gives us the privilege of being an integral part of it. Lydia gave her home for the mission of serving the early church as a host and place where all could meet and share their gospel stories.

Are you in collaboration with the Savior? Has He given your life purpose? May we find fulfillment in Him as we serve Him in ways He presents to us or opens the doors for us to walk through with Him.

If God has already given my life purpose when He created all, why am I still concerned about it? He has given me purpose and as I live this life, He will reveal it to me. As I look to Him to be led, His handiwork in me will happen.

✦

> "BUT WHEN HE, THE SPIRIT OF TRUTH, COMES, HE WILL GUIDE YOU INTO ALLTHE TRUTH." - JOHN 16:13A

**Reflect on the truths of God in Lydia's life.**
What are the truths of God that you learned from Lydia's life and story?
How do you see them applying in your own life?

# LYDIA

DAY SIX - WHAT ARE GOD'S TRUTHS?

# A PERSPECTIVE
## A SYNOPSIS

Each Biblical character has a purpose in scripture. God speaks to us through their stories and shows Himself to us. Notice the character of God through His showing up, speaking, His actions, and His ways. He teaches us through these persons in history, our forefathers in the faith.

As God shows us who He is through the scripture, He also does so in our lives. He is the same yesterday, today, and forever. We notice something today because our hearts are drawn by His Holy Spirit to this aspect of God Himself. Tomorrow it may be a different, yet not a less important attribute of who God is. We cannot get to the end of God. He reveals Himself as He chooses; He loves us and draws us near with each part of Himself. To know Him is to let ourselves go into His open heart and arms ready to embrace us. Within the stories of the people of God, there are as many ways God uses as there are persons. He uniquely comes and brings each of us close to enfold us to Himself. However, He remains as the person of God He says He is; we can count on it.

God has the long view, not only eternally, but also for the generations. God shows us Himself through the generational stories in scripture. So often, the Lord instructs one to do a certain thing and instead they would go their own way. For example, Moses confused his abilities or lack of them as reasons for not following God's commands. Out of his misguided notion for God and worship, David followed his own heart, not God's, in pursuing the building of the temple. Paul determined to spread the gospel and was so headstrong that he turned several relationships into train wrecks. However, God, full of mercy and compassion, uses whom He chooses; each of these people of God were His vessels, also full of sin. God overcomes our sin through Jesus Christ for His name and the generations that follow us; He uses our inabilities or our failures to further His purposes for all the world to know Him.

In the persons from scripture, we see our enduring Heavenly Father and Almighty Savior at work in their lives and find applications to ours.

*Looking back at our own, we delve into the life of another of God's children in God's word*
Let's take a look back at our history. What are a few of the milestones in your life: graduations, moves, work, marriage, divorce, children, death, loss, and other significant time periods? Imagine that God was with you as you walked through each of these milestones. He was there when you graduated and started the new job. He was there when you met your future spouse, and He was there when you were let go from your dream job. Were you aware that He was with you through it all?

We find that our Biblical persons too had milestones, some of which they could celebrate, but often there were times of pain. We can see some of the ways God was preparing them to reach out, to cry out to God, and we can also see why they were grateful for the times that were good. God is the giver of all good things; He does not withhold anything from His own (Psalm 84:11).

Each of us has a past with good and not so good in it; the characters of the Bible do too. Some of them we know little about, but we can be certain that it is also true of them. The first part of the Bible includes much about Moses. We know his history: born of a Hebrew slave but raised by Pharaoh's wife, fluent in all things Hebrew and Egyptian, murdered an Egyptian, wandered in the desert, to name a few. As we read his story, we can see many facets of his life and conclude that the reason God chose him to lead the Israelites was because he had the right history and it certainly appears so. However, God chose him because God chooses. God was sovereign over all the events in Moses' life just as He is in ours. Our history is not separate from our Creator God; it is a woven tapestry. We make decisions and choices as Moses did, but God uses all in the life of one who follows Him for His purposes (Romans 8:28). Moses' life became the vessel God chose for the leadership of His people.

God chooses whom He chooses, and He chooses well. We often have the misguided notion that God chooses us because of something we are or do; similarly, we think we earn the right to be chosen. On the other hand, we may think God does not choose us because of something we have or have not done. While God is righteous and just, He is also merciful and compassionate. He is sovereign over all. He chooses us because He loves us. He also allows our choices in all matters, whether good or not. Our histories, complete with poor decisions and choices, become the means by which God works in our lives and the lives of others too. He works all into good for us and for His glory; He uses our broken places to show the world His great love. It is mystery and grace and truth, all in one. God is not only the God of the improbable, but He also is the God of the impossible.

God does this very thing with each of us as we follow Him. When we collaborate with Him, He builds a life and a story, which will be one for His purposes and His renown, a means by which the world will know Him. With each character and story in His word, God gives us many insights into the life of a child of God and the story He has written on their lives. God is writing each of ours too. Why not review your milestones from the perspective of the hand of God on your life. He was there, and He is with you now.

Our heavenly Father of all creation and Savior God is trustworthy; we can trust Him with all that concerns us. We are His, and He has given us His all in order for us to live with Him forever. It is not something we earn or achieve but a gift, greater than we imagine. God wants a real relationship with each of us, His creation for His purpose on this earth at such a time as this. His name is over all creation. He is God; there is no other. All creation cries out to Him.

We cry out to Him because He first made us to do so. He knows our cries before we utter them (Isaiah 65:24). We can be certain that if He wants us to know who He is and what He does, He will give us the ability to know Him and walk with Him.

The most amazing part to me is that the great God of the universe has made Himself accessible to us. He comes to us for us to know Him, to be lifted up into a relationship with Him. Jesus provides the way to our heavenly Father. His Holy Spirit opens our hearts, eyes, and ears to know Him. He then carries us across the threshold to know His rescue, to receive His grace, and to walk with Him through the storms and trials, and to persevere in the waiting and the suffering.

We need Jesus. Oh, we need Jesus to carry on, to make it through, and most importantly of all, to receive all there is of Himself. And the only way we will receive the abundance He has to offer us is to have His help to do so. We cannot do it on our own. He rescues us to Himself as He makes Himself known to us and we make the choice to allow His rescue and the ongoing life that follows. He carries us through the failures and the hardships of leaving the old behind; He watches over us as we enter the new life; he fights our battles and helps us surrender our dreams and our all to Him; He takes our broken places and in them He gives us a new rendering, a new whole. The Lord Jesus comes to us right where we are. His heart for us gives us hope and eyes to see, ears to hear, and a heart to know Him, who carries us across all thresholds, which were once barriers but now are doors to life and life to the full.

We have to experience our broken places, know our sin and our hard heartedness in order to know our need for Jesus Christ. And as we choose to follow Him, we must remember our need for Him. He will help us in the trenches where we are. Are we willing to allow His rescue? If we receive and acknowledge the need and move toward the light, we will be rescued by our Savior Jesus. We are not able to do anything on our own. We only think we can. God knows the way; He loves our company. To cross over into His new, enter new, receive new, and live the new life, we know we need Him and invite Him in and collaborate with Him.

The mountain which is I becomes the very means God uses to get through to me; He moves me aside so that He can lead the way. I must allow Him to do it. As I do, the new view may or may not come immediately, but when He leads, I know the way is true. He becomes more; I become less. His presence is palpable, and the relief is real. I know that He is God; there is no other. His rescue releases me from the snare of myself. As we read about the real people in the Bible and the new way God chose for them to illustrate who He is and what He does, we see that their lives are not so different from yours and mine. Perhaps the times seem different, but the human beings are not. The brokenness, the sin, and controversies in relationships are all the same. But perhaps the most illuminating part of all of it is that God reveals Himself through their stories. God is the same yesterday, today, and forever.

# FINAL THOUGHTS

Would you consider writing your thoughts about your journey with God and the truths you have learned as you studied the twelve men and women from God's word in this Bible study? You may write it as a prayer of gratitude for the One and Only, who authored each of these stories and your own. Please use the space below to write your prayer or thoughts about the truths of God in His word.

*Consider making a new commitment to the Lord, the author of your story, to praise Him
for the wonder of His great love, to move with Him in ways you never dreamed,
and to be the child He created you to be in this world for such a time as this
so that the world may know Him, who was, and is, and will be beyond our imagination.*

*Well done, reader and student of God's word.
I so appreciate going on the walk with you and
pray that you will know Him more and more.
May you be mightily blessed by the truths
of God as you continue on the journey with Him.*